Good Cook's
MICR⦵WAVE

Good Cook's
MICROWAVE

Everything your oven would tell you
is better cooked in the microwave

CAROLYN HUMPHRIES

foulsham
LONDON • NEW YORK • TORONTO • SYDNEY

foulsham

The Publishing House, Bennetts Close,
Cippenham, Berkshire, SL1 5AP, England

ISBN 0-572-02586-6

Printed in Great Britain by Cox & Wyman Ltd, Reading, Berkshire

Introduction

Your microwave is probably the most efficient and versatile tool in your kitchen. If you are only using it for defrosting and reheating foods, then you know that you are not getting the best out of it – there's far more it can do, and many tasks it performs better than a conventional oven. So the first thing to remember is that your oven and your microwave are not in competition – they are in partnership. The trick is to learn to use them in conjunction with each other.

As a labour- and fuel-saving device, the microwave is second to none. There's less washing up, too, as many foods can be cooked and served in the same dish, and when cooked in the microwave, foods notorious for causing horrible saucepans – such as porridge or scrambled eggs – leave the bowls just needing a quick wash out. You'll cut out penetrating cooking smells and there'll be no more walls streaming with condensation either!

You will find all kinds of tasks – such as skinning fruit, toasting nuts, drying breadcrumbs, cooking vegetables – can be done simply and quickly in the microwave, with the minimum of mess. You will also find that many things cook more quickly in the microwave, making it a bonus when time is of the essence.

This book will tell you, at a glance, everything you need to know to get the most out of your microwave. It has cooking and thawing times, recipes, technical know-how and handy hints. It tells you what to do and what not to do. It highlights the benefits and identifies the pitfalls. Its dictionary format and easy-to-read text will make it an invaluable source of information. Everything is arranged alphabetically, with cross-references provided to help you find exactly what you want to know. Types of food that require similar treatment, such as vegetables, are grouped together for quick and easy reference. You will also find delicious recipes listed under individual entries.

Good Cook's Microwave strips away the mystery and turns it into magic. So keep a copy by your oven, dip into it every time you need quick, sensible advice, and make your microwave really work for you.

Notes on the Recipes

Dotted through the book you'll find useful recipes for everything from a basic white sauce to a sponge pudding. To get the best results, please read the following before use.

- When following a recipe use either the metric, imperial or American measures; never mix them up.
- All spoon measures are level: 1 tbsp = 15 ml, 1 tsp = 5 ml.
- All eggs are medium unless otherwise stated.
- Make sure any dish you use is suitable for microwaving (➤ *see Dishes, page 37*).
- Don't add salt before cooking.
- Season and flavour foods sparingly before cooking as microwaving intensifies flavour.
- Cooking times are given in a range from the shortest time for 900–1000 watt cookers to a longer time for 600 watt cookers. But remember, microwaving is not an exact science. Cooking times should be used as a guide only. <u>Always cook for the shortest time given</u>, then check the result and add on a little more time if necessary – we may be talking just a few seconds!
- Different microwaves use different terms for the power output settings. I have used High, Medium-High, Medium, Medium-Low and Low. ➤ *See Power Output Settings, page 89,* for the other terms used, if yours are different from these.
- Use your microwave in conjunction with your conventional cooker. For instance, if you are making Spaghetti Bolognese, it may be more convenient to cook the meat in the microwave while cooking the spaghetti conventionally, so that both are ready at the same time.

Experiment. The more you use your microwave, the more you will discover what it can do for you.

Aduki beans

> *see Pulses, page 90*

Agar-agar

Made from seaweed, it is a setting agent. The powdered form is the easiest to use. Use 10 ml/2 tsp per 600 ml/1 pt/2½ cups liquid (that includes any cream or fruit purée in a recipe). Put the agar-agar in a bowl and add 150 ml/¼ pt/⅔ cup of the liquid from the recipe. Stir, then microwave on High for 1 minute or until the mixture boils. It must actually boil for the setting agent to work. Cool slightly, then use as required.

Almonds

> *see Nuts, page 79*

Antennae

> *see Paddles, page 82*

Apples

> *see Fruit, page 47*

Apple sauce   Prepare as for stewed fruit (> *see page 47*) but add a knob of butter and beat well once cooked to form a fairly smooth purée.

Apples, baked   Select fairly large, even-sized fruit. Wash, dry and cut out the central cores. Do not peel. Arrange in a circle in a round casserole dish (Dutch oven). Fill the cavities with one of the following fillings: brown sugar; a mixture of brown sugar, dried mixed fruit (fruit cake mix) and a pinch of mixed (apple-pie) spice; chopped glacé (candied) cherries and a pinch of ground cinnamon; golden (light corn) syrup or jam (conserve) of your choice. Cover with a lid and cook on High for about 2 minutes per apple, depending on size, or until the fruit is just tender.

Apricots

> *see Fruit, page 47*

Apricots, dried

> *see Fruit, Dried, page 48*

Arcing

Metallic utensils, large pieces of foil or crockery with gold or silver trim should not be used in the microwave oven as they reflect microwaves and will produce a blue spark called arcing. If arcing occurs, turn off the microwave immediately as it can cause serious damage to the cooker's magnetron (➤ *see page 69*).

Arcing can also occur when very small amounts of food are being cooked. To stop this happening, place a small cup of water in the cooker with the food. This will absorb some of the microwave energy and prevent this happening.

➤ *see also Foil, page 46*

Arranging foods for cooking

It is best to arrange pieces of food on a dish in a circle with the centre left empty to allow the microwaves to penetrate the food from the centre as well as the outside. If you are cooking uneven-sized foods such as chicken legs, broccoli or chops, arrange them in a single layer with the densest parts (the meaty part of chops or chicken legs or the stalks of broccoli) facing outwards.

Arrowroot

Arrowroot can be used as a thickener like cornflour (cornstarch). It is particularly good for making a clear, thickened juice for spooning over fruit as a glaze. But, unlike cornflour and flour, the starch grains do not need cooking once brought to the boil. Blend with the liquid to be thickened (the juice from a can of fruit, for instance) – 30 ml/2 tbsp will thicken 300 ml/½ pt/1¼ cups liquid – and cook on High until thickened and clear, stirring frequently. Do not continue to cook or the mixture will go runny again.

Artichokes, globe

➤ *see Vegetables, pages 115–19*

Artichokes, Jerusalem

➤ *see Vegetables, pages 115–19, and Jerusalem Artichokes, page 60*

Asparagus

➤ *see Vegetables, pages 115–19*

Aubergines (eggplants)

➤ *see Vegetables, pages 115–19*

Avocados

If you overcook avocados, they become bitter. To serve cooked as a starter, slice half a ripe avocado per person and arrange in individual shallow dishes. Spoon just enough passata (sieved tomatoes) over to cover. Sprinkle with a pinch of dried basil and a little salt and freshly ground black pepper. Top with a thin layer of grated Mozzarella cheese. Microwave on High just until the cheese melts, no longer. Serve straight away.

Avocado soup Make 900 ml/1½ pt/3 cups chicken or vegetable stock in a large bowl, using 2 stock cubes and boiling water, and microwave on High for 2 minutes. Meanwhile, scoop the flesh of 2 large avocados into a blender or food processor and add 15 ml/1 tbsp lemon juice, 30 ml/2 tbsp snipped chives, a little salt and pepper and a few drops of Tabasco sauce. Run the machine until smooth. Whisk the avocado mixture into the hot stock and microwave for a further 2 minutes. Ladle into warm bowls and add a small spoonful of crème fraîche to each before serving.

Baby food

Commercial jars of baby food can be heated in the microwave. Remove any metal caps, cover the jar with kitchen paper (paper towels) and microwave on High for 20–30 seconds. Stir well, check the food is not too hot and serve.

Babies' bottles   Do not sterilise babies' bottles in a microwave.

Baby food, home-cooked   If you reheat home-made baby food in the microwave, you must make it piping hot, then let it cool down; never just warm it or you could cause food poisoning. Always check it has cooled enough before giving it to your baby.

Baby milk (formula)   Place a 200 ml/7 fl oz bottle of milk, with teat cover still on, in the microwave. Heat on High for 30–45 seconds. Shake thoroughly to disperse the heat evenly. Test the temperature before feeding.

Bacon

Cooking bacon joints   ➤ *see Meat, page 72*

Cooking rashers (slices)   For best results, lay the rashers on a microwave rack (➤ *see page 75*) over a plate. Cover with greaseproof (waxed) paper to prevent spitting. Microwave on High for 30 seconds to 1 minute per rasher, depending on thickness. Leave to stand for 2 minutes before serving. If you don't have a rack, lay the rashers on a sheet of greaseproof paper on a plate and cover with a second sheet, then continue as above. You can also use a browning dish (➤ *see page 19*). For crispy bacon, to crumble as a topping or use in sandwiches, place streaky rashers on a sheet of kitchen paper (paper towel) with another sheet laid loosely over the top. Cook for a few seconds more per rasher until crisp and brown.

Baked beans

To heat through, empty the can into a bowl. Cook on High for 1 minute. Stir, then continue to heat, stirring at 1 minute intervals, until piping hot. A 400 g/14 oz/large can will take 2–3 minutes.

Baked beans on toast   Make the toast in the usual way and spread lightly with butter or margarine. Place on a plate and spoon cold baked beans on top. Microwave on High for 1 minute. Cook 1 portion at a time.

Baking

> see Apples, page 7, Bread, page 16, and Eggs, page 41

Baking parchment

> see Non-stick Baking Parchment, page 79

Bananas

> see Fruit, page 47

Butterscotch baked bananas Put a large knob of butter or margarine in a round, shallow dish. Add 30 ml/2 tbsp light brown sugar and 15 ml/ 1 tbsp lemon juice. Lay a sheet of kitchen paper (paper towel) over the top to prevent splattering and cook on High for 1 minute. Remove the paper and stir well to blend. Peel 2 bananas and halve lengthways. Cut each length in half. Arrange in a single layer in the dish and turn the bananas over to coat with the sauce. Cover with kitchen paper again. Cook on High for 2½–3 minutes until the bananas are just soft but still hold their shape. Serve hot with cream or ice cream.

Basil

> see Herbs, Drying, page 55

Baskets

Bread, rolls, croissants and brioches can be warmed briefly in a basket in the microwave before serving. However, do not use baskets for prolonged cooking or they will burn.

> see also Warming Bread, page 17

Bastes

Brush any of these over poultry or a joint of meat, both before cooking and once or twice during cooking, to enhance colour and flavour.

Red baste Melt 25 g/1 oz/2 tbsp butter or margarine in a bowl, covered with a piece of kitchen paper (paper towel), on High for about 30 seconds. Stir in 15 ml/1 tbsp tomato ketchup (catsup), 10 ml/2 tsp paprika and 5 ml/1 tsp each of Worcestershire sauce and soy sauce.

Brown onion baste Melt 25 g/1 oz/2 tbsp butter or margarine as for Red Baste (above) and stir in 5 ml/1 tsp dried onion granules, 15 ml/1 tbsp Worcestershire sauce, 5 ml/1 tsp soy sauce and a good grinding of black pepper.

Barbecue baste Melt 25 g/1 oz/2 tbsp butter or margarine as for Red Baste (➤ *see page 12*) and stir in 15 ml/1 tbsp tomato purée (paste), 15 ml/ 1 tbsp clear honey, 15 ml/1 tbsp brown table sauce, 2.5 ml/½ tsp garlic purée and 5 ml/1 tsp malt vinegar.

Bay leaves
➤ *see Herbs, Drying, page 55*

Beans, dried, all types
➤ *see Pulses, page 90*

Beans, fresh, all types
➤ *see Vegetables, pages 115–19*

Beansprouts
➤ *see Vegetables, pages 115–19*

Béarnaise sauce
➤ *see Sauces, Egg-based, page 98*

Beef
➤ *see Meat, pages 71–4*

Beefburgers
➤ *see Burgers, page 21*

Beetroot (red beets)
➤ *see Vegetables, pages 115–19*

Bell peppers
➤ *see Peppers, page 84*

Biscuits (cookies)
Crisp biscuit recipes don't work well. But a microwave is ideal for making sticky bars like flapjacks or crumbly ones like shortbread that are cooked in a slab, then cut into fingers.
➤ *see Flapjacks, page 45, and Shortbread, page 101*

Biscuit base Melt 50 g/2 oz/¼ cup butter or margarine in a fairly large bowl, covered with a sheet of kitchen paper (paper towel), on High for 1 minute. Stir in 175 g/6 oz/1½ cups biscuit crumbs, then press into the sides and base of an 18 cm/7 in flan dish (pie pan). Cook on High for 2 minutes, leave to cool, then chill before filling.

Refreshing stale biscuits Plain biscuits or crackers that have gone slightly soft can be made crisp once more by arranging in a circle, in a single layer on a sheet of kitchen paper (paper towel) on the turntable or base of the microwave. Heat on High for 10–20 seconds. Leave to cool (they will crisp as they cool), then store in an airtight container.

Biscuits

> *see Scones, page 100*

Blackberries

> *see Fruit, page 47*

Blackcurrants

> *see Fruit, page 47*

Blanching nuts

> *see Nuts, page 79*

Blanching vegetables

> *see Vegetables, page 119*

Block margarine

> *see Butter, page 22*

Blue cheese

> *see Cheese, page 26*

Blueberries

> *see Fruit, page 47*

Boil-in-the-bag packs

These may be cooked from frozen following the manufacturer's instructions. Remember to pierce the bag in two or three places on top so it does not burst. Make sure the food is piping hot throughout before serving.

> *see also Labelling, page 63*

Boiling

You can boil pasta, rice and vegetables in the microwave. You need less water than cooking conventionally. Do not boil eggs in their shells in the microwave as the shells will explode.

> *see also Pasta, page 82, Rice, page 94 and Vegetables, page 115*

Bolognese sauce

Put a chopped onion, 350 g/12 oz minced (ground) meat and a crushed garlic clove in a large bowl. Microwave on High for 4–5 minutes, stirring once or twice until the meat is no longer pink and all the grains are separate. Add a 400 g/14 oz/large can of chopped tomatoes, 15 ml/1 tbsp tomato purée (paste), 30 ml/2 tbsp red wine (optional), 2.5 ml/½ tsp dried oregano, 5 ml/1 tsp caster (superfine) sugar and a little salt and freshly ground black pepper. Cook on High for 15–20 minutes, stirring once or twice until a rich sauce has formed. Cover and leave to stand for 5 minutes before serving. Serves 4.

Spaghetti Bolognese   Either cook the pasta conventionally while the sauce is cooking, or cook in the microwave while the Bolognese Sauce is standing – it won't matter that it stands a few minutes longer.
     ➤ see also Cannelloni, page 25, Lasagne, page 65, and Pasta, page 82

Bottling fruit

Prepare a sugar syrup (➤ see page 107); use light for sweeter fruits, heavy for tart fruits. Sterilise the preserving jars (➤ see Sterilising, page 105). Pack each jar with fruit and fill up the jars with the prepared syrup. Cover with microwave-safe clingfilm (plastic wrap) and cook one jar at a time on High for 2–3 minutes or until the syrup is boiling. Turn the power down to Medium-Low and cook for a further 3–4 minutes. Remove from the oven using oven gloves. Cover, seal and label.

Braising or pot-roasting

A small joint of topside or silverside benefits most from this method of cooking. Weigh the joint. Use your conventional recipe but reduce the liquid by half. Cover and cook on High until the liquid boils. Turn the power down to Medium and cook for 30 minutes per 450 g/1 lb. Turn the meat over halfway through cooking. Ideally use a microwave thermometer (➤ see page 75) to check the meat is fully cooked. Leave to stand for 15 minutes. Taste and re-season the juices, if liked, before serving.

Brazil nuts

     ➤ see Nuts, page 79

Bread

All types of bread may cooked in the microwave, but wholemeal bread will have a better colour than white. Bread crust will not brown or crisp, so after cooking place the loaf under a hot grill (broiler) for a few minutes on each side to finish off the crust. Alternatively, brush before cooking with a little beaten egg and sprinkle with toasted sesame seeds, poppy seeds, whole grains or rolled oats to enhance the appearance.

Baking bread   First, warm your flour. Put the measured flour in a large bowl and cook on High for about 2 minutes until warmed through. Stir, then continue with your normal recipe until the dough is ready to prove. Put the kneaded dough in a large bowl, cover with a clean cloth or kitchen paper (paper towels) and cook on High for 10–15 seconds only. Leave to stand for 5 minutes. Repeat this process five or six times until the dough has doubled in bulk. Knock back (punch down). Turn into a microwave loaf container or other suitably shaped dish. Prove as before. Cook until the dough is well risen, spongy and shrinking slightly from the edge of the container. A 450 g/1 lb loaf will take 4½–6 minutes on High.

Garlic bread   Mash 50 g/2 oz/¼ cup butter or margarine with 1–2 crushed garlic cloves and 15 ml/1 tbsp chopped parsley. Cut a small baguette into 12 slices, not right through the bottom crust. Spread the butter mixture between the slices and smear any remaining over the top. Wrap in greaseproof (waxed) paper. Microwave on Medium for 1–2 minutes or until the butter has melted into the bread. Don't overcook or the bread will toughen as it cools.

Quick granary bread   Mix 350 g/12 oz/3 cups granary bread flour, 10 ml/2 tsp bicarbonate of soda (baking soda), 5 ml/1 tsp cream of tartar and 5 ml/1 tsp salt in a bowl. Rub in 50 g/2 oz/¼ cup butter or margarine. Stir in 200 ml/7 fl oz/scant 1 cup cultured buttermilk and enough milk to form a soft but not sticky dough. Shape into a round on a lightly floured surface. Place on a large, well-oiled dinner plate. Mark deeply in quarters with a knife, not cutting right through. Cook on High for 6–9 minutes. The dough will rise and spread and feel spongy to the touch. Leave to stand for 10 minutes, then transfer to a wire rack to cool completely. Pull into quarters and cut into thick slices. Eat while fresh.

Refreshing stale bread   Cut into slices if the loaf is uncut. Wrap in kitchen paper (paper towels) and microwave on High for 10 seconds for each 6 slices. Don't overcook or the bread will toughen.

Soda bread Cook as for Quick Granary Bread (≻ *see page 16*), but use half white and half wholemeal flour instead of granary flour.

Thawing bread Wrap uncut loaves in kitchen paper (paper towels) and microwave on High for 1½–2 minutes. Leave to stand for 5 minutes to finish thawing out the centre. Don't continue to heat or you'll toughen the bread.

Leave cut loaves wrapped, but remove any metal ties. Microwave on Low for 4–5 minutes until the loaf feels just soft when gently squeezed. Turn over halfway through.

To thaw a few slices only, wrap in kitchen paper (paper towels) and microwave on High for 10–15 seconds. Turn over halfway through.

Note: you can toast single slices straight from frozen.

To thaw rolls, croissants, bagels and buns, place on kitchen paper (paper towels) – in a ring if thawing several at once – and cover with kitchen paper. Microwave on Medium-Low for 8–10 seconds per item. Leave to stand for 2–3 minutes. To serve warm, add 5 seconds per item. You can place them in a ring on a napkin in a basket, ready for serving, if liked.

Warming bread To warm fresh slices of bread for serving, wrap in kitchen paper (paper towels) and microwave on High for about 10 seconds per item. Test and add a few seconds longer, if necessary. Do not overheat or they will be tough. Brioches, croissants, fruit buns, pitta breads, rolls, etc., can be warmed in the same way.

Bread and butter pudding

Prepare in your normal way, using 600 ml/1 pt/2½ cups milk. Cook on Medium-Low for 25–30 minutes until lightly set. Place under a preheated grill (broiler) to brown and crisp the top. Leave to stand for 5 minutes before serving.

Bread sauce

Make enough white breadcrumbs to three-quarters fill a small microwave-safe bowl. Stir in just enough milk to cover the crumbs. Peel a small onion and press a clove into it. Push down into the soaked crumbs and sprinkle with a little salt, freshly ground black pepper and grated nutmeg. Cover with kitchen paper (paper towels) and microwave on High for 1½–2 minutes. Stir and microwave for a further 2–3 minutes. Leave to stand for at least 15 minutes to let the flavours develop. Remove the onion, add a little more milk if the sauce is too thick and microwave for a further 30 seconds to 1 minute until thoroughly heated before serving.

Breadcrumbs

To dry breadcrumbs, make crumbs in the usual way in a blender or food processor (including the crusts). Spread 100 g/4 oz/2 cups crumbs on a large plate. Microwave on High for about 3–4 minutes, stirring every minute until completely crisp. Store in an airtight container.

Breadcrumbs, buttered and toasted Put 15 g/½ oz/1 tbsp butter or margarine in a bowl, cover with a sheet of kitchen paper (paper towel) and microwave on High for 10–20 seconds. Stir in 50 g/2 oz/1 cup fresh breadcrumbs. Spread half on a plate and microwave on High for 1 minute. Stir well and microwave for a further 1–1½ minutes until crisp. Tip into a container. Repeat with the remaining crumbs.

Breadcrumbs, flavoured and toasted Prepare as for Buttered and Toasted Breadcrumbs (above) but flavour to taste with garlic or onion granules, celery salt, curry or chilli powder. For sweet crumbs, add 5 ml/ 1 tsp granulated sugar and a pinch of mixed (apple-pie) spice, ground cinnamon or grated nutmeg and toss well.

Breakfast cereal

Stale breakfast cereal can be revived in the microwave. Spread stale cereal on a large plate (a minimum of 1 portion, preferably more). Cook on High for 30 seconds, then stir. Continue to cook in 30-second bursts until the cereal feels crisp. Cool, then store in an airtight container.

> ➣ *see also Granola, page 52, and Porridge, page 86*

Brie

> ➣ *see Cheese, page 26*

Brioches

> ➣ *see Bread, page 17*

Broccoli

> ➣ *see Vegetables, pages 115–19*

Brown rice

> ➣ *see Rice, page 94*

Browning agents

Many people are put off microwaving foods because they don't brown. The simplest way to overcome this is to use a browning dish (➣ *see page 19*). If you do not have a browning dish, many dishes can be placed under a hot grill (broiler) for a few minutes to brown and crisp.

There are also many other methods which have the advantage of adding extra flavour:

Browning meat and poultry   Before cooking, brush with:
- Melted butter or oil followed by a good dusting of paprika
- Warm honey, mixed with a good dash of soy sauce and a generous squeeze of lemon juice
- Any of the following mixed with an equal quantity of water
    Mushroom or tomato ketchup (catsup)
    Worcestershire sauce
    Soy sauce
    Brown table sauce
    Barbecue sauce
OR halfway through cooking, brush with:
- Redcurrant jelly (clear conserve)
- Shredless marmalade
- A mixture of clear honey and wholegrain or Dijon mustard
Alternatively, before cooking in the microwave, quickly sear and brown the surfaces of meat or poultry in a frying pan (skillet).

Browning cakes and breads   Again there are several choices:
- Use wholemeal flour rather than white (you may need a little extra liquid) and/or brown sugar instead of white (chocolate or coffee cakes look fine anyway).
- Substitute 15 g/½ oz/2 tbsp custard powder for white flour to improve the colour.
- Before cooking cakes in the microwave, sprinkle the surface with ground cinnamon, chopped nuts, desiccated (shredded) coconut or chopped glacé (candied) fruits.
- Halfway through cooking cakes, sprinkle with a mixture of demerara or light or dark brown sugar and chopped, toasted nuts.
- After cooking, dust cakes with sifted icing (confectioners') sugar or coat in butter cream, icing (frosting) or melted chocolate.
- Before cooking breads or rolls, brush with egg yolk and sprinkle with cracked wheat, toasted sesame seeds or poppy seeds.
- Before cooking scones (biscuits), brush with melted butter, then sprinkle savoury ones with toasted sesame seeds and sweet ones with chopped nuts or demerara sugar.

Browning dish

This is a specially designed microwave dish which absorbs microwave energy. It can be used to sear and cook meat, poultry, sausages, eggs and even pizzas and toasted sandwiches. It has to be preheated in the microwave for several minutes before using. Always follow the manufacturer's instructions, use oven gloves when handling after heating and don't place it directly on your work surface as it gets extremely hot. Reheat the dish for half the original time if cooking batches of food.

Preheat the dish for 4–8 minutes, according to your microwave output. Add a knob of butter or 15 ml/1 tbsp oil and swirl round. Add the food to be cooked, pressing it down on the plate, thinnest parts towards the centre. Cook on High for times stated below:

Using a browning dish

Type of food	Preparation	Quantity	Cooking time
Chips (fries)	Spread evenly.	2 portions	3–6 minutes, turning once.
Chops	Sprinkle with dried herbs, if liked.	2 large or 4 small	4–6 minutes, turning once.
Fish fingers	Cook from frozen.	4 fingers	2–3 minutes, turning once.
Fish cakes	Cook from frozen.	4 cakes	4–6 minutes, turning once.
Fried eggs	Prick the yolk with a cocktail stick (toothpick).	4 eggs	3–4 minutes on Medium
Gammon/ ham steaks	Snip edges with scissors to prevent curling.	2 medium	3–5 minutes, turning once.
Hamburgers	Don't grease the dish.	2 quarter pounders or 4 small	2–4 minutes, turning once.
Liver	Cut into thin slices, add freshly ground black pepper.	8 thin slices	2–3 minutes, turning once.
Potato waffles	Cook from frozen.	2 large or 8 small	3–4 minutes, turning once.
Pizza	Cook from frozen.	1 small	4–6 minutes
Sausages	Prick with a fork, don't grease the dish.	8 chipolatas 8 large	2–4 minutes 4–6 minutes, turning once
Steaks	Add steak seasoning or a sprinkling of dried herbs.	2 × 225 g/8 oz	4–8 minutes, turning once.
Toasted sandwiches	Butter the bread on the outside, don't grease the dish.	2 rounds	2–3 minutes, turning once.

Browning element

Some microwaves have a built-in browning element which works like a grill (broiler). Follow the manufacturer's instructions for use.

Brussels sprouts

➤ *see Vegetables, pages 115–19*

Bulgar (cracked) wheat

Put 225 g/8 oz/2 cups bulgar wheat in a deep dish. Microwave on High for 2–3 minutes, stirring until lightly toasted. Add 600 ml/1 pt/2½ cups boiling water and cook on High for 4–5 minutes until fluffy and the water is absorbed, stirring twice during cooking. Season to taste. Serves 4–6.

➤ *see also Tabbouleh, page 109*

Burgers

Burgers containing meat of any kind are best cooked conventionally but they can be cooked from frozen in the microwave. Place on a microwave rack (➤ *see page 75*) over a plate to catch any fat. Cover with greaseproof (waxed) paper and microwave on High for 30–45 seconds per burger. Turn over and microwave for a further 30–45 seconds, check, and continue in 20-second bursts, if necessary, until the burger just turns from pink to brown in the centre, but is not drying at the edges. Leave to stand for 30 seconds before serving. A browning dish (➤ *see page 19*) can be used.

Quorn burgers These cook very well in the microwave, but are best cooked from frozen. Brush with oil, place on a rack and cover with greaseproof (waxed) paper. Cook on High for 30–45 seconds per burger. Turn over and cook a further 30 seconds to 1 minute or until piping hot through.

Note: Three or four burgers will take only a little longer than two.

Veggie burgers Cook as burgers containing meat.

Burning

Burning foods Most foods don't burn, they simply dry out and become unpalatable. But those with a high sugar or fat content, such as chocolate or pastry (paste), can get extremely hot and burn in places. So always cook in short bursts and check frequently so that foods don't overcook.

Burning yourself Microwaves can't burn you because the cooker automatically switches itself off when you open the door. Microwave-safe dishes, too, don't get heated by microwaves. But dishes can get hot by the conduction of heat from the food to the dish and if a dish in unsuitable for the microwave (such as ironstone pottery) it will absorb microwaves and become hot. So, as a precaution, use oven gloves when lifting cooked dishes out of the oven. Browning dishes (➤ *see page 19*) become intensely hot, so always protect your hands.

Butter

Hard butter and block margarine can be softened straight from the fridge. Place on a plate and microwave on Medium-Low for 30 seconds to 1 minute, then leave to stand for 2 minutes. If not quite soft enough to spread, give extra bursts of 10 seconds, testing each time. Do not overheat or it will melt.

To melt butter or margarine, place in a bowl. If melting more than 25 g/1 oz/2 tbsp, cut into cubes. Cover the bowl with kitchen paper (paper towels) and microwave on High until just melted (about 20–30 seconds for 25 g/1 oz/2 tbsp).

Flavoured butters The following can be used to drizzle over plain cooked meat, fish, poultry or vegetables as a garnish before serving. In each case, for 4 servings, melt 50 g/2 oz/¼ cup butter or margarine in the microwave:

Citrus: add the finely grated rind and juice of ½ orange and ½ lemon. Season with freshly ground black pepper.

Garlic: add 1 large, crushed garlic clove, 15 ml/1 tbsp chopped parsley and a good grinding of black pepper.

Maître d'hôtel: add 30 ml/2 tbsp chopped parsley and a squeeze of lemon juice.

Tarragon: add 30 ml/2 tbsp chopped tarragon and 5 ml/1 tsp brandy.

➤ *see also Bastes, page 12*

Unsalted (sweet) butter It is not vital to use this in preference to ordinary butter, but it is particularly good for brushing foods before cooking to help enhance their colour and flavour.

Cabbage

➤ *see Vegetables, pages 115–19*

Cakes, fruit

Make in your normal way but use dark brown sugar and a few drops of gravy browning for extra colour. Always make a hollow in the centre to ensure the cake cooks through – or use a microwave ring container and have a ring-shaped cake! Wrap the cake in foil for the standing time to help the cooking process. Cook on Medium-Low. Check after 10 minutes and then at 1-minute intervals until beginning to shrink from the sides of the container. When done, the cake feels just firm to the touch and a cocktail stick (toothpick) inserted in the centre comes out clean. There may still be moist spots on the top.

Christmas cake   To make a Christmas cake, use your usual recipe. Don't add alcohol to the mixture before cooking – use fruit juice or milk instead and add an extra 15 ml/1 tbsp for each egg used. When cold, pierce well on both sides with a skewer and pour 15–30 ml/1–2 tbsp brandy or rum over each side (or use orange juice if you prefer). Wrap in a double thickness of foil and store for at least 1 month to mature.

Cakes, sponge

Small and large sponge cakes of most kinds can be cooked in the microwave with excellent results. Remember these general rules:

- They won't brown, so for plain cakes substitute 15 g/½ oz/2 tbsp custard powder for the same quantity of self-raising (self-rising) flour and add an extra 1.5 ml/¼ tsp baking powder to the mixture.
  OR
  Use light brown sugar instead of caster (superfine).
  OR
  Use wholemeal flour instead of white.
- Make the mixture slightly wetter than when cooking conventionally: add an extra 15 ml/1 tbsp milk for every egg used.
- Don't grease the container if plastic. If pottery or Pyrex is used, grease it very lightly and base-line the container with greaseproof (waxed) paper or non-stick baking parchment. Do not over-grease or flour the container or it will give an unpleasant crust to the cake.

- Do not overcook. The cake will rise considerably and should still have damp spots on the top. These will dry out during standing time. If overcooked, it will be completely dry.
- The cake is cooked when it is risen and is beginning to shrink away from the sides of the container.
- When making a chocolate sponge, don't use more than 15 g/½ oz/ 2 tbsp cocoa powder to every 100 g/4 oz/½ cup butter or margarine, or the cake will be heavy.
- Always stand the cake container on a microwave rack (➤ see page 75) or an upturned small plate for cooking. This helps to distribute the microwaves more evenly.
- Never cover a cake when cooking.
- The cake will not be harmed if it sinks when you check after the shorter cooking time. It will rise up again as soon as you continue to cook it.
- For small fairy cakes, make up half the quantity of Basic Sponge Cake mixture (➤ see below). Arrange 6–7 double-thickness paper cake cases (cupcake papers) in a circle on a plate and place on an upturned small plate or microwave rack. Half-fill with the sponge mixture. Microwave on High for 1½–3 minutes, turning and rearranging once after 1 minute. Cool on a wire rack.

Basic sponge cake Sift 85 g/3½ oz/good ¾ cup self-raising (self-rising) flour, 15 g/½ oz/2 tbsp custard powder and 5 ml/1 tsp baking powder into a bowl. Add 100 g/4 oz/½ cup light brown sugar, 100 g/4 oz/½ cup soft, tub margarine and 2 eggs. Beat well with a wooden spoon or electric beater until smooth. Beat in a few drops of vanilla essence (extract) and 30 ml/ 2 tbsp milk. Turn into an 18 cm/7 in microwave cake container or very lightly greased deep, round dish, base-lined with non-stick baking parchment. Stand the dish on a microwave rack or upturned small plate and microwave either on High for 4–6 minutes or Medium-High for 5–8 minutes until beginning to shrink from the sides but still with a few moist spots on top. Leave to stand for 10 minutes, then turn out on to a wire rack to cool completely. Split and fill with jam (conserve), butter cream or whipped cream and fresh fruit, as required.

Chocolate cake Make as for Basic Sponge Cake (above), substituting cocoa (unsweetened chocolate) powder for the custard powder.

Coffee cake Make as for Basic Sponge Cake (above), adding 15 ml/ 1 tbsp instant coffee, dissolved in the milk.

Camembert

➤ see Cheese, page 26

Candied fruit

➤ *see Fruit, Glacé, page 48*

Cannelloni

Prepare a Bolognese Sauce (➤ *see page 15*) and use to fill 8 no-need-to-precook cannelloni tubes. Place in a dish, cover with Cheese Sauce (➤ *see page 99*) and microwave as for Lasagne (➤ *see page 65*).

Capsicums

➤ *see Peppers (Bell), page 84*

Carrots

➤ *see Vegetables, pages 115–19*

Cashews, roasting

➤ *see Nuts, page 79*

Cassata

➤ *see Ice Cream, page 57*

Casseroles

Don't use tough cuts of meat, as you would for a conventional casserole: the result will be disappointing. But poultry, game and tender cuts of meat, such as chops or steaks can be 'casseroled' in a sauce very successfully and vegetarian casseroles based on pulses work beautifully.

Cook any onion or vegetables in a little oil in a casserole dish (Dutch oven) for 1–2 minutes until slightly softened. Brown the meat conventionally in a frying pan (skillet), then add to the vegetables with the liquid and flavourings (but don't use more than 300ml/½ pt/1¼ cups liquid to 450 g/1 lb meat. Cook on High until the liquid boils, then turn down to Medium and cook for 30 minutes per 450 g/1 lb meat. Test, then cook in 3-minute bursts until cooked through. Lift out the meat, cover and leave to stand while you thicken the juices. Blend a little cornflour (cornstarch) with water. Stir into the juices, return to the microwave and cook on High for 2 minutes until thickened. Stir again, return the meat to the casserole, microwave on High for 1 minute to reheat, and serve.

Cauliflower

➤ *see Vegetables, pages 115–19*

Celeriac (celery root)

➤ *see Vegetables, pages 115–19*

Celery

> see Vegetables, pages 115–19

Celery root

> see Vegetables, pages 115–19

Chapattis

To warm in the microwave, place two at a time on a microwave rack (> see page 75) or plate, and microwave on High for 45 seconds to 1 minute until puffy and hot.

Cheese

To ripen soft cheese, such as Camembert, Brie or blue cheese   Place on a plate. Microwave on Medium-Low for 15 seconds to 1 minute depending on the size and how unripe the cheese is, until the cheese is just softening, not running! Leave to stand for 5 minutes before serving.

To soften soft cheese and cheese spread   Place in the microwave in its container (removing all foil coverings) and cook on Medium-Low for 5–15 seconds only. Leave to stand for 1 minute before spreading.

Cheese fondu   Mix a crushed garlic clove with 225 g/8 oz/2 cups each of grated Gruyère or Emmental (Swiss) cheese and 225 g/8 oz/2 cups grated Cheddar cheese in a large bowl. Add 25 g/1 oz/¼ cup cornflour (cornstarch), a little salt and freshly ground black pepper and 1.5 ml/¼ tsp grated nutmeg. Measure 300 ml/½ pt/1¼ cups white wine and 300 ml/½ pt/1¼ cups milk in a measuring jug. Add 15 ml/1 tbsp kirsch. Cook on Medium-High for 2–4 minutes until the mixture is hot but not boiling. Gradually blend into the cheese mixture. Return to the microwave and cook on Medium-High for 9–12 minutes or until smooth and bubbling, stirring twice. Serve hot with cubes of French bread. Serves 4–6.

Cheese on toast   Make toast in the usual way and spread with butter or margarine, if liked. Place on a plate. Top with an even layer of thinly sliced or grated cheese. Microwave on High for 15–45 seconds, until the cheese has just melted. Do not overcook or the whole thing will become hard.

Cheese sauce

> see Sauces, Milk-based, page 99

Cheesecakes, thawing

Remove any foil container. Place on a plate. For a 15 cm/6 in cake, cook on Medium-Low for 2–3 minutes only. For a 20–23 cm/8–9 in cake, cook on Medium-Low for 3½–6 minutes only. You must then leave it to stand for 30 minutes to defrost completely. Do not try to defrost more quickly.

Cherries
> ➤ *see Fruit, page 47*

Chestnuts
> ➤ *see Nuts, page 79*

Chick peas (garbanzos)
> ➤ *see Pulses, page 90*

Chicken
> ➤ *see Poultry and Game, pages 86–8*

Chicory (Belgian endive)
> ➤ *see Vegetables, pages 115–19*

Braised chicory Cut a cone-shaped core out of the base of 4 heads. Thickly slice the heads and place in a casserole dish (Dutch oven). Dot with 25 g/1 oz/2 tbsp butter or margarine. Cover and cook on High for 1½–2 minutes or until the fat melts. Toss to mix. Crumble in ½ chicken or vegetable stock cube, 30 ml/2 tbsp water, 5 ml/1 tsp dried onion granules and 5 ml/1 tsp lemon juice, then stir, cover and cook on High for 7–10 minutes, stirring twice. Leave to stand for 2 minutes, then serve. Serves 4.

Chilli con carne

Put 350 g/12 oz minced (ground) beef or lamb in a large bowl with 1 chopped onion and 2.5 ml/½ tsp chilli powder (or to taste), 5 ml/1 tsp ground cumin and 2.5 ml/½ tsp dried oregano. Microwave on High for 3–5 minutes, stirring twice, until the meat is no longer pink and all the grains are separate. Stir in a drained 425 g/15 oz/large can of red kidney beans, a 400 g/14 oz/large can of chopped tomatoes and 15 ml/1 tbsp tomato purée (paste). Cover with kitchen paper (paper towels) to prevent splattering and cook on High, stirring every 5 minutes for 15–25 minutes until cooked and a rich sauce is formed. Season to taste. Leave to stand for 5 minutes, then serve with flour tortillas or plain boiled rice, shredded lettuce and grated Cheddar cheese. Serves 4.

Note: For larger appetites, add an extra can of drained kidney beans and cook for an extra 1–2 minutes, if necessary.

You can use home-cooked beans (➤ *see Pulses, page 90*) if you wish. 100 g/4 oz/⅔ cup dried beans is equivalent to a 425 g/15 oz/large can.

Chinese leaves (stem lettuce)

These are usually served as a salad ingredient but can either be shredded to cook in a stir-fry (➤ *see page 105*) or cooked like cabbage (➤ *see Vegetables, page 116*).

Chips (fries)

You can buy specially prepared microwave chips. Follow the manufacturer's instructions. Oven chips can be cooked on a browning dish (➤ *see page 19*).

Chives

> ➤ *see Herbs, Drying, page 55*

Chocolate

To melt chocolate, break up 100 g/4 oz/1 cup chocolate and place in a bowl. Microwave on Medium for 2–3 minutes, stirring and checking every 30 seconds until melted. Do not overheat or it will burn.

Chocolate cake

> ➤ *see Cakes, Sponge, page 23*

Chocolate chip ice cream

> ➤ *see Ice Cream, page 57*

Chocolate fudge icing

> ➤ *see Icing, page 58*

Chocolate sponge pudding

> ➤ *see Sponge Puddings, page 103*

Chops

> ➤ *see Meat, pages 71–4*

Choux pastry (paste)

You can't cook choux pastry in a microwave, but you can reheat it.
> ➤ *see Pastry (paste), pages 82–3*

Christmas pudding

You can use your normal recipe, but use only 30 ml/2 tbsp alcohol. Replace the rest with apple or orange juice (a high alcohol content could make the pudding burn). First, put the fruit in a large bowl and add the alcohol and juice. Cover with a plate. Microwave on High, checking and stirring every minute, until the fruit is hot and plump and has absorbed the liquid. Leave to cool. Then add the remaining ingredients and add an extra 15 ml/1 tbsp milk for every egg used. Turn into very lightly greased basins, base-lined with non-stick baking parchment. Cover with greaseproof (waxed) paper – do not use foil – and microwave one pudding at a time on a microwave rack (➤ *see page 75*) or upturned small plate on Medium for 20–40 minutes until the top is just slightly moist. Leave to stand for 5 minutes, then turn out and serve. Alternatively, leave until cold, cover with clean greaseproof paper and store in a cool place for up to 2 weeks.

To reheat Cook the pudding on Medium for 6–12 minutes until hot through. Turn out and serve sprinkled with caster (superfine) sugar and decorated with a sprig of holly.

To reheat one portion Put the slice in a bowl. Cover with a saucer or small plate. Microwave on Medium for 30 seconds to 1½ minutes until piping hot.

Chutney

Use your normal chutney recipe. Sterilise the jars (➤ *see Sterilising, page 105*). Put the prepared ingredients in a large bowl and cook on High for 30 minutes. Stir well, then continue to cook in 5-minute bursts until thick and pulpy. Pot, cover and label.

➤ *see also Safety, page 97*

Cilantro

➤ *see Herbs, Drying, page 55*

Citrus fruit

➤ *see Fruit, Citrus, page 48*

Cleaning your microwave

Always wipe up any spills straight after use or they will attract the microwaves next time you cook, which could affect the cooking time. Microwaves don't differentiate between food to be cooked and gruesome leftovers! After cooking or cleaning, wipe out the inside with a dry cloth or kitchen paper (paper towels) to remove any condensation which may cause rust in time. Make sure door seals are also kept clean or microwaves could escape.

   To freshen the interior (after cooking fish, for instance), put a bowl containing about 300 ml/½ pt/1¼ cups water, a few slices of lemon and a clean cloth. Cook on High for 3–5 minutes until boiling. Leave until lukewarm, then squeeze out the cloth and wipe all over the inside. Dry with a dry cloth or kitchen paper.

Clingfilm (plastic wrap)

It is no longer recommended that you use normal clingfilm in your microwave. It has been found that the diezethylhexledipate (DEHA) used in the manufacture to give it its elasticity can pass into food during cooking, although it is not known to what degree this may be harmful. Some makes that don't use DEHA as a plasticiser can be used and this is stated clearly on the packaging. If there are no instructions for use in the microwave, do not use it.

➤ *see also Covering Foods, page 33*

Coatings

Because foods don't brown in the microwave, a coating is often needed to make food look more appetising. Chops, steaks or poultry portions can be dipped first in beaten egg and then in dried or toasted breadcrumbs (➤ *see page 18*), toasted nuts (➤ *see page 80*) or sesame seeds (➤ *see page 101*), crushed crisps (potato chips), cornflakes or branflakes or stuffing mix before cooking. Alternatively, they can be basted or glazed.

➤ *see also Bastes, page 12, and Browning Agents, page 18*

Coconut

Coconut can be toasted in the microwave. For best results put desiccated (shredded) coconut in a roaster bag. Tie up, then microwave on High, until golden, shaking twice.

➤ *see also Nuts, page 80*

Cod

➤ *see Fish, page 43*

Coffee

Making ground coffee Put 10 ml/2 tsp ground coffee per person in a jug. Pour in one cupful of cold water per person. Heat on High until beginning to froth on top but not quite boiling – about 1–1½ minutes per cup. Stir once halfway through heating. Remove from the microwave, leave to stand for 2 minutes, then draw a cold spoon across the surface. This will settle the grounds. Pour as usual.

Making instant coffee Pour cold water, milk, or half milk and half water into a cup or mug. Heat until just boiling. Stir in the granules or powder. Add a dash of cold milk, if liked.

Reheating a mug of coffee ➤ *see Reheating, page 94*

Coffee cake

➤ *see Cakes, Sponge, page 23*

Coffee ice cream

➤ *see Ice Cream, page 57*

Cold spots

➤ *see Hot and Cold Spots, page 56*

Collard greens

➤ *see Vegetables, pages 115–19*

Confectioners' custard

➤ *see Sauces, Milk-based, page 99*

Conserve

➤ *see Jam, page 59*

Containers

➤ *see Dishes, page 37*

Convenience foods

Many ready-made foods such as pizzas, baked beans, canned pasta, soups and stews, frozen and cook-chill meals can be reheated in the microwave. Follow the manufacturer's instructions on the can or packet. Always remove any foil containers and empty canned foods into a bowl. Stir canned foods several times during heating to distribute the heat evenly. Remember always to pierce the bag of boil-in-the-bag foods.
➤ *see also Reheating, page 94, and individual entries.*

Converting conventional recipes

➤ *see Recipe Conversion, page 92*

Cook-chill foods

Follow the instructions on the packet. If no microwave instructions are given, it is probably unsuitable for cooking in this way.
➤ *see also Labelling, page 63*

Cooker settings

➤ *see Power Output Settings, page 89*

Cooking times

Cooking times vary from microwave to microwave, depending on the output of the oven. In this book, the times are given as a guide to the range of outputs from the highest (900–1000 watt) to the lowest (600 watt). When microwave ovens were first available, many had an output as low as 500 watts. These are not common now, so I have not included them. If you do have such a low-output cooker, use the longest cooking times given in the book and add on an extra 20 seconds for every minute. Whatever your oven output, always cook for the shortest time given, then check and cook a little longer if necessary. The more you use your microwave, the more you will get used to the times required for specific tasks in your model – they all vary!

In some cookery books, the recipes have been tested using just one output – older books may use 600 watts, newer ones 750–850 watts. The very latest may use 900–1000 watts. The high wattage cookers (750/850 –1000 watts) are so fast that just a few seconds will make a great difference, so cook for the shorter time, check and cook for a few seconds more if necessary.

Adjusting times for lower wattage ovens To change from a 600 watt oven to a 650/700 watt oven, decrease cooking time by up to 20 seconds per minute.

To change from 650/700 watts to 750/850 watts, decrease cooking time by up to 20 seconds per minute.

To change from 600 watts to 750/850 watts, decrease cooking time by up to 40 seconds per minute.

Notes: The cooking times when using Medium-Low or Low settings vary very little whatever the power output.

If you have a 900–1000 watt cooker, you may find you get better results for some foods by cooking on Medium-High for a little longer than on High. Trial and error is the only way to find out.

Equivalent cooking times

750–1000 watts	650–700 watts	500–600 watts
20 secs	30 secs	40 secs
50 secs	1 min	1 min 30 secs
2 mins 30 secs	3 mins	4 mins
4 mins	5 mins	6 mins 30 secs
8 mins 30 secs	10 mins	13 mins 30 secs
12 mins 30 secs	15 mins	20 mins
16 mins 30 secs	20 mins	27 mins
20 mins	30 mins	40 mins

➣ *see also Power Output Settings, page 89, and Labelling, page 63*

Coriander (cilantro)

➤ *see Herbs, Drying, page 55*

Corn (on the cob)

➤ *see Vegetables, pages 115–19*

Cottage pie

➤ *see Shepherd's Pie, page 101*

Courgettes (zucchini)

➤ *see Vegetables, pages 115–19*

Courgettes with garlic Slice 2–3 courgettes. Place in a bowl with a knob of butter or margarine and a crushed garlic clove. Cook on High for 4–6 minutes, stirring twice, until just tender. Season with salt and freshly ground black pepper. Leave to stand for 3 minutes. Serves 4.

Couscous

Put 600 ml/1 pt/2½ cups water and a chicken or vegetable stock cube in a large bowl. Microwave on High until boiling. Stir to dissolve the cube. Add 225 g/8 oz/1⅓ cups couscous and 30 ml/2 tbsp olive oil. Cook on High for 2–6 minutes until swollen and all the liquid is absorbed. Fluff up with a fork and leave to stand for 5 minutes. Fluff up again and serve immediately. Serves 4.

Covering foods

As a general rule, foods which need to be covered when cooking conventionally need to be covered when microwaving. Clingfilm (plastic wrap) was used in the past but it is now known that many types are not suitable for using in the microwave. Specially-made microwave covers are widely available, however, and there are many other methods:

- A dome of greaseproof (waxed) paper or a piece of kitchen paper (paper towel) is ideal to prevent foods splattering.
- When cooking dishes containing liquids, a plate that fits over the bowl or container, or a casserole dish (Dutch oven) with a lid is best.
- Don't cover cakes or breads when cooking.
- Don't use foil for covering as it is metallic. However, small strips can be used to mask ends of food which may burn or dry out during cooking e.g. wing tips or bone ends (➤ *see Shielding, page 101*).
- Roaster bags can also be used. They are good for poultry and joints. They help to brown the food as well as preventing splattering and they also keep the food moist. Tie with a plastic (not metal) tie, string or an elastic band. If you are roasting a joint and you don't want it to 'stew',

place the bag containing the joint in a casserole dish (Dutch oven) and pierce the bag underneath so the excess juices drain into the dish. Alternatively, if there's room, put the joint on a microwave rack (➤ *see page 75*) or upturned plate inside the bag; or put the joint in the pierced bag, on the rack or upturned plate over a large plate to catch the juices.

- Non-stick baking parchment is suitable for freezing as well as microwaving so is good for lining dishes or covering food to be cooked, then frozen or vice versa.

Crab

➤ *see Fish, page 43*

Crackling

If your crackling on roast pork hasn't 'crackled', cut it off the joint, place on a microwave rack (➤ *see page 75*) over a plate and cover with a piece of kitchen paper (paper towel). Microwave on High for 1–3 minutes until you hear it pop and sizzle. Remove the paper. If it hasn't bubbled all over, return for a few seconds more. Cool slightly so it hardens, then serve.

Cranberries

➤ *see Fruit, page 47*

Cranberry sauce   Put 225 g/8 oz cranberries in a bowl with 150 ml/¼ pt/ ⅔ cup water and 100 g/4 oz/½ cup sugar. Cover and microwave on High for 2–3 minutes until the fruit is 'popping'. Stir well. Turn down to Medium and cook, uncovered, for a further 6–8 minutes until a rich sauce is formed. Taste and add more sugar if liked.

Cream, thawing

For a 250 ml/9 fl oz carton of whipped or double (heavy) cream: remove any foil from the container. Microwave on Medium-Low for 2½–3 minutes. Leave to stand for 5 minutes, then stir gently and serve. Note: Single cream is not suitable for freezing as it will curdle on thawing.

Cream cakes, thawing

15 cm/6 in cake   Place on a piece of kitchen paper (paper towel) on a plate. Microwave on Medium-Low for 3–4 minutes. Leave to stand for 1 hour to complete defrosting.

20 cm/8 in cake   Microwave on Medium-Low for 5–6 minutes. Leave to stand for 2 hours before serving. Do not try to increase the defrost time or you will ruin the cake!

Eclairs   Place 4 éclairs in a circle on kitchen paper (paper towels) on a plate. Microwave on Medium-Low for 45 seconds to 1 minute. Leave to stand for 10 minutes. Do not attempt to defrost more quickly or the cream and chocolate will melt completely.

Crème caramel

For the caramel, put 90 ml/6 tbsp granulated sugar and 30 ml/2 tbsp hot water in a bowl. Stir well. Microwave on High for 3–6 minutes until golden brown. Pour into four ramekin dishes (custard cups). Whisk 3 eggs with 30 ml/2 tbsp caster (superfine) sugar and 450 ml/¾ pt/2 cups milk. Add a few drops of vanilla essence (extract), to taste. Pour into the ramekins and place in a large, shallow, round dish. Pour hot water into the flan dish to come halfway up the sides of the ramekins. Cook on Medium for 16–20 minutes until the custard has set. Leave to cool, then chill for at least 3 hours or preferably overnight before turning out to serve. Serves 4.

Crisping

It is not possible to crisp the skin on poultry, meat, etc. successfully in the microwave. Once cooked, place under a hot grill (broiler) to brown.

However, it is possible to crisp items such as biscuits (cookies), ➢ *see page 13*, and stale breakfast cereals (➢ *see page 18*) which have become soggy, by drying them in the microwave. A similar process is used to dry breadcrumbs (➢ *see page 18*), herbs (➢ *see page 55*) and flowers (➢ *see page 46*).

Croissants

➢ *see Bread, page 17*

Croûtons

Cut the crusts off 3 slices of bread and cut the bread into small cubes. Place in a single layer on a plate. Microwave on High for 4–6 minutes, tossing every minute until crisp and dry.

Garlic croûtons   Toss the bread in 5 ml/1 tsp garlic granules or garlic salt before cooking.

Crumb coatings

➢ *see Coatings, page 30*

Crumbles

Fruit or savoury crumbles can be made in the microwave but the topping will not crisp or brown. For a better texture, you can add chopped nuts and use wholemeal flour and demerara sugar instead of white. A crisper savoury crumble can be made using dry stuffing mix or toasted breadcrumbs (➤ *see page 18*), instead of the normal flour and fat crumble. To crisp and brown the surface, place briefly under a preheated grill (broiler) after cooking.

To help prevent fruit juice bubbling over a sweet crumble, stir 5 ml/ 1 tsp cornflour (cornstarch) into every 225 g/8 oz prepared fruit. Do not add extra water to the fruit in the dish.

Crystallised (candied) fruit

➤ *see Fruit, Glacé, page 48*

Curds

Lemon curd is the most common, but you can also make curd with oranges or limes. Sterilise the jar (➤ *see Sterilising, page 105*). Use your normal recipe but make only 450 g/1 lb at a time. Put the fruit rind and juice, the sugar and butter in a large bowl. Microwave on High for 2–3 minutes until hot. Stir, then whisk in the eggs. Microwave on High for a further 4–6 minutes, whisking after every 30 seconds, until thick and smooth. Do not allow to boil. If it seems to be getting too hot before it thickens, reduce the power to Medium and continue as before. Pot, cover and label in your usual way.

Curly kale

Cook as for spring (collard) greens (➤ *see Vegetables, page 117*).

Curry

You can make curries in a microwave but do not use tougher cuts of meat.

Quick curry sauce This is good served over eggs, poultry, sliced cooked meat or fish. Empty a 295 g/10½ oz/medium can of condensed celery or mushroom soup in a large bowl and stir in 90 ml/6 tbsp water. Stir in 30 ml/2 tbsp tomato purée (paste), 5 ml/1 tsp garlic purée, 5 ml/1 tsp dried onion granules, 15 ml/1 tbsp curry paste, 5 ml/1 tsp garam masala, 5 ml/1 tsp ground turmeric, 30 ml/2 tbsp mango chutney and 50 g/2 oz creamed coconut. Cover and microwave on High for 2 minutes. Stir and heat for a further 2 minutes. Stir again and heat until the coconut is melted and the mixture is bubbling. Thin with a little more water. Season to taste. Serves 4–6.

Custard

➤ *see Sauces, Milk-based, page 99*

D

Damsons

➤ *see Fruit, page 47*

Defrosting

➤ *see Thawing, page 109*

Desserts

➤ *see individual entries*

Dill (dill weed)

➤ *see Herbs, Drying, page 55*

Dishes

The following are suitable for use in a microwave: ovenproof glass dishes, specially made microwave ware, glazed earthenware, dishwasher-safe porcelain, pottery and boilable plastic. You can also use basketware and wood but only for very short cooking times (➤ *see Warming Bread, page 17*). Do not use metal bakeware, ironstone, thin plastics or any crockery with metal trim.

The dish test   To test if a container is suitable for microwave cooking, stand half a cup of water in the dish to be tested. Microwave on High for 1 minute. If the dish feels cool but the water is hot, it is suitable for use. If the dish feels hot and the water is cool, the dish absorbs microwaves and should not be used.

Shape and size   Round, oval or rectangular dishes with rounded corners give the best results, because the microwaves are distributed more evenly. If the dish is too small, the food could bubble over and take longer to cook as it is so dense. If the dish is too big, the food may become dry and overcook.

A shallow dish of food will cook more quickly than a deep one. Choose straight-sided containers and, if a lid is going to be needed, a casserole dish (Dutch oven) is ideal.

For vegetables, choose a dish large enough to hold them in a single or shallow layer.

For a recipe cooked in liquid, such as a casserole, allow about 5 cm/ 2 in space above the ingredients to allow enough room for it to boil.

For cakes and bread, give enough height of dish for rising.

Dough

> see Bread, page 16, and Pizza, page 84

Doughnuts

There are now several brands of microwave-and-serve doughnuts. Cook according to the manufacturer's instructions.

Refreshing jam doughnuts Day-old doughnuts can be softened by microwaving on Medium for 20 seconds per doughnut. Take care, the jam will be hot!

Thawing cream doughnuts Place on a plate on a piece of kitchen paper (paper towel). Microwave on Medium-Low for 20–25 seconds per doughnut. Check halfway through. If the cream is beginning to melt, remove from the microwave. Leave to stand for at least 5 minutes or until soft, then put in the fridge for a few minutes to chill the cream, if liked.

Thawing jam doughnuts Place on a plate on a piece of kitchen paper (paper towel). Cook on Medium-Low for about 45 seconds per doughnut, or 2½ minutes for 4 doughnuts. Leave to stand for 2 minutes.

Dried fruit

> see Fruit, Dried, page 48

Drinking chocolate

Fill a mug with cold milk, leaving a 2.5 cm/1 in headspace. Microwave on High for 1–2 minutes until almost boiling and beginning to froth on the top. Remove and sprinkle on drinking (sweetened) chocolate powder, to taste. Whisk with a fork or small wire whisk until blended and frothy.

Drying herbs

> see Herbs, Drying, page 55

Drying flowers

> see Flowers, Drying, page 46

Duck

> see Poultry and Game, pages 86–8

Dumplings

These can be placed around the top of a casserole for the last 5–8 minutes' cooking time or can be cooked separately.

Mix 100 g/4 oz/1 cup self-raising (self-rising) flour with 40 g/1½ oz/ ⅓ cup shredded suet and a pinch of salt. Stir in 15 ml/1 tbsp chopped parsley or other herbs. Mix with enough cold water to form a soft but not sticky dough. Knead gently and shape into six small balls. Place in a circle on a sheet of greaseproof (waxed) paper. Microwave on High for 4–6 minutes until fluffy and set. Leave to stand for 1 minute before serving.

Crispy dumplings Brush the balls of dough with water and coat in stuffing mix or chopped, toasted nuts (➤ *see Nuts, page 80*), before cooking.

Dying fabrics

Wearing rubber gloves, empty a 100 g/4 oz container of Dylon Natural Dye into a large bowl. Stir in 200 ml/7 fl oz/scant 1 cup cold water, using a plastic or wooden stirrer, until the dye is completely dissolved. Blend in a further 400 ml/14 fl oz/1¾ cups cold water. Add the fabric and push down well until completely submerged. Dye only 225 g/8 oz of cotton or linen at one time. (Synthetic fabrics won't work and of course you can't dye any clothes with metal zips or fasteners.) Put the bowl in a large roaster bag and tie with string. Microwave on High for 3–5 minutes. Remove from the cooker. Carefully open the bag and pour away the liquid. Rinse the fabric in cold water until the water is clear. Wash in warm suds, then dry away from direct heat.

Tie-dying Knot the fabric in several places, by tying it with string or elastic bands or knotting it with itself. Immerse in the dye and continue as before. Untie before drying.

E

Eclairs, thawing

> see Cream Cakes, Thawing, page 34

Egg custard

Prepare as for Crème Caramel (> see page 35), but omit the caramel. Cook in one larger dish instead of ramekins (custard cups) if liked.

Eggplants

> see Aubergines, page 8, and Vegetables, pages 115–19

Eggs

Contrary to popular belief, eggs cook beautifully in a microwave – but a little care must be taken not to overcook them.

Baked eggs For all power outputs: place a small knob of butter or margarine in each of up to four ramekins (custard cups) and melt for a few seconds in the microwave on High. Break an egg into each dish. Prick the yolks in two or three places with a cocktail stick (toothpick) to prevent bursting. Top each with 5 ml/1 tsp double (heavy) or whipping cream. Arrange the ramekins in a circle in the microwave. Bake for 15 seconds per egg on High. Stand for 1 minute, then bake again for a further 20 seconds per egg. Leave to stand again before serving.

Boiled eggs Do not attempt to boil eggs in their shells or they will explode. Special containers for 'boiling' eggs in the microwave are obtainable.

Fried (sautéed) eggs To fry 1 egg, use a browning dish (> see page 19), or oil or lightly butter a saucer. Break the egg on the saucer and pierce the yolk two or three times with a cocktail stick (toothpick). Cover with a plate. Cook on High for 30 seconds. Leave to stand for 1 minute. Cook for a further 15–30 seconds or until the white is just set. Leave to stand for 1 minute to complete cooking.

For 2 eggs, use an oiled or greased shallow dish instead. Cook as above for 1 minute on High, stand for 1 minute, then cook for a further 20–40 seconds until the whites are just set. Don't try to fry more than two eggs at once.

Omelettes Melt a small knob of butter or margarine in a small, round, shallow dish for a few seconds on High. Beat 3 eggs with a good pinch of salt and a generous grinding of black pepper and 30 ml/2 tbsp cold water until just blended, not frothy. Pour into the dish. Cover with a plate. Cook on High for 1½ minutes. Stir gently to bring the cooked mixture towards the centre and add flavourings such as grated cheese, fresh chopped herbs, etc., if liked. Cook again for a further 1 minute. Remove the plate and cook for a further 30 seconds to 1½ minutes until completely set. Fold over, slide out of the dish and serve.

Poached eggs For all power outputs. Put about 2.5 cm/1 in boiling water into each of up to four ramekin dishes (custard cups). Break an egg into each one. Pierce the yolks in two or three places with a cocktail stick (toothpick). Place in a circle in the microwave. Cook on High for 30 seconds per egg. Leave to stand for 2 minutes to complete cooking, then carefully drain off the water and slide out of the cups, on to plates, to serve.

Scrambled eggs Use up to 8 eggs. Break in a bowl and beat well. Beat in 15–30 ml/1–2 tbsp milk per egg. Add a knob of butter or margarine and a little salt and freshly ground black pepper. Microwave on High for 45 seconds to 1 minute per egg, stirring after each minute. Remove from the oven while still slightly runny as the egg will continue to cook. Leave to stand for 2 minutes before serving.

Soufflé omelette Separate 4 eggs. Beat the yolks with 30 ml/2 tbsp water. Season with a little salt and freshly ground black pepper or sweeten with 5 ml/1 tsp caster (superfine) sugar. Whisk the egg whites until stiff and fold in with a metal spoon. Lightly butter a 20 cm/8 in round, shallow dish. Spoon in the egg mixture. Cook on Medium for 5–8 minutes, until puffy and just set. Fold in half and serve straight away, either plain or with a sweet or savoury sauce of your choice.

En papillote

This cooking method (literally 'in paper') is particularly well suited to cooking fish. Put the fish, either whole or a fillet, with flavourings on a double thickness of non-stick baking parchment or greaseproof (waxed) paper, lightly greased with butter or margarine. If using a whole fish, slash in several places on each side. Wrap securely and place on a plate. Microwave on High for 3–5 minutes or until the fish is just tender. Leave to stand for 2 minutes. Transfer to a serving plate and open at the table. To cook two parcels, allow 5–8 minutes, for four parcels, arrange in a circle on a large plate and cook for 6–10 minutes.

F

Fennel

> see Vegetables, pages 115–19

Fish

Fish can be cooked to perfection in the microwave, remaining moist and full of flavour. For best results, follow these general rules:

- Fish cooks very quickly so take great care not to overcook. This is particularly true of shellfish.
- It is best to remove fish from the oven when the larger flakes are still translucent. Cover and leave to stand for a few minutes and the fish will complete cooking.
- Always slash whole fish in two or three places on each side before cooking to ensure even distribution of the microwaves.
- Cook smoked fish in the same way as plain (see below).
- Cover any thin tails with a small strip of smooth foil to protect against overcooking.
- Do not add salt before cooking.

Cooking pieces of fish Remove the skin, if preferred, and lay the pieces in a shallow dish in a single layer, thinnest parts towards the centre. Either dot with butter or margarine or add 30 ml/2 tbsp liquid (wine, milk, cider, water or stock) per portion. Add a sprig of fresh herbs or a bay leaf, if liked. Cover and microwave on High. Allow 3½–6 minutes per 450 g/1 lb for thin fillets and tail pieces, and 5–7 minutes per 450 g/1 lb for thick fillets and steaks. Leave to stand for 2 minutes, then carefully lift the fish out of the liquid. If liked, thicken the liquid with a little cornflour (cornstarch) blended with milk or water and cooked on High for 1–2 minutes, stirring once. Add cream or crème fraîche, if liked, and season to taste.

Flat fish (plaice, sole, halibut) Lay the fish in a single layer in a shallow dish or cook one at a time. Dot with butter or margarine and sprinkle with lemon juice. Cover and cook on Medium for 3–5 minutes per fish until just tender. Leave to stand for 2–3 minutes before serving.

Kippers Cook as for thin pieces of fish (> see above).
> see also Boil-in-the-bag Packs, page 14

Lobster and crab Do not cook live lobster or crab in the microwave.

Moules marinière   Chop an onion. Place in a large bowl or casserole dish (Dutch oven). Add a knob of butter or margarine. Cover and microwave on High for 2–3 minutes. Stir once. Add 1 kg/2¼ lb scrubbed and bearded mussels and 150 ml/¼ pt/⅔ cup white wine. Cover and cook on High for 2–5 minutes, stirring twice, until the shells have opened. Discard any that have not. Sprinkle with chopped parsley and serve in large soup bowls. Serves 2.

Mussels   Scrub and remove beards, discarding any that are damaged or open. Place in a large casserole (Dutch oven) with 150 ml/¼ pt/⅔ cup water or white wine. Cover and cook on High for 2–5 minutes, stirring after every minute until the shells are open. Discard any that remain closed.

Prawns (shrimp) or scallops   Place in a shallow dish and add a little butter or margarine or liquid (➤ *see Cooking Pieces of Fish, page 43*). Cover and cook on Medium for 2–3 minutes per 225 g/8 oz, stirring once or twice. Leave to stand for 2 minutes before serving. Cook until just pink for prawns, or until scallops go milky white.

Roes   Prick the membranes of 225 g/8 oz roes in several places. Lay in a single layer in a lightly buttered or oiled dish. Cover and cook on High for 2–3 minutes. Turn over and cook for a further 1–3 minutes or until cooked through. Season, leave to stand for 2 minutes and serve, sprinkled with lemon juice and chopped parsley.

Round fish (trout, mackerel, herring)   Slash the fish in two or three places on each side. Lay head to tail in a shallow dish. Dot with a little butter or margarine and sprinkle with lemon juice. Cover and cook on High for 4–6 minutes per 450 g/1 lb, carefully turning over once after 3 minutes' cooking time.

Soused herrings or mackerel (rollmops)   Remove the heads and tails from 4 cleaned herrings or mackerel. Open out and place skin-sides up on a board. Run your thumb up and down the backbone to loosen. Turn the fish over and lift off the backbone and any remaining bones. Roll up the fish, skin-sides out, and place in a single layer in a shallow dish. Sprinkle with 1 chopped or thinly sliced onion, 15 ml/1 tbsp light brown sugar, 8 peppercorns, 2 bay leaves and 10 ml/2 tsp pickling spice. Pour over 300 ml/½ pt/1¼ cups cider or white wine vinegar. Cover and cook on High for 8–12 minutes, rearranging the fish once after 5 minutes. Leave to cool in the liquid. Chill before serving.

➤ *see also En Papillote, page 42*

Fish, frozen

Fish cooks well from frozen, but cook fillets and whole fish on Medium instead of High, allowing an extra 1–2 minutes per 450 g/1 lb.

Fish cakes To cook frozen fish cakes, place on a lightly oiled plate, in a circle. Cover and cook on High for 45 seconds to 1¼ minutes per cake, turning once. Crisp under a preheated grill (broiler) briefly, if liked, or use a browning dish (➤ *see page 19*).

Fish fingers These can be cooked from frozen but the coating will go soft. Arrange in a circle on a lightly oiled, round plate. Microwave on High for 30 seconds to 1 minute per fish finger, turning once. Crisp briefly under a hot grill (broiler) if liked, or preferably, use a browning dish (➤ *see page 19*).

Flageolet beans

➤ *see Pulses, page 90*

Flambéing

Warm spirits for flambéing in the microwave WITH CARE. Always measure the spirit and place in a small, flameproof bowl. Microwave on High for no more than 15–20 seconds per 30 ml/2 tbsp. Ignite and pour over the food to be flambéed.

Flan case (pie shell)

➤ *see Biscuit Base, page 13, and Pastry (paste), page 82*

Flans

➤ *see Pastry (paste), page 82, and Quiches, page 92*

Flapjacks

Grease a shallow rectangular dish about 15 × 20 cm/6 × 8 in. Put 75 g/3 oz/⅓ cup butter or margarine in a bowl with 50 g/2 oz/¼ cup light brown sugar, 30 ml/2 tbsp golden (light corn) syrup and 2.5 ml/½ tsp mixed (apple-pie) spice. Microwave on High for 1 minute. Stir and microwave for 1 further minute. Stir in 175 g/6 oz/1½ cups rolled oats. Press into the prepared dish. Place the dish on a microwave rack and microwave on High for 2–3 minutes or until the mixture feels just firm. Leave to stand for 5 minutes, mark into fingers, then leave to cool completely in the dish before removing. Makes about 15 fingers.

Flavourings

The flavour of all foods is intensified when microwaved, so don't season heavily before cooking. Use herbs, spices, garlic and other seasonings sparingly – you can always add more, but you can't take them out! Don't add salt before cooking.

➤ *see also Salt, page 97*

Flour

Using wholemeal flour instead of white will enhance the colour of breads, pastry (paste) and cakes that do not brown.

Warming flour ➤ *see Bread, page 16*

Flour tortillas

➤ *see Pancakes, page 82*

Flowers, drying

Petals dry more successfully than whole heads. Arrange them in a single layer on a sheet of kitchen paper (paper towel). Cook on High for 1 minute. Turn them over and cook on High for 1 further minute or until the petals are dry. Tip into a bowl and add a few drops of pot pourri oil for added fragrance.

Foil

Use foil sparingly. Small smooth strips can be used to shield wing tips, bone ends or thin parts of food that would otherwise overcook or dry out. If you use too much or it is too crumpled, arcing (➤ *see page 8*) will occur. This can damage the cooker.

Use foil, shiny side in, to cover food when standing to encourage final cooking. It is ideal, for instance, to wrap individual, jacket-baked potatoes. They will then keep hot for up to an hour.

Fondant fruits

➤ *see Icing, page 58*

Fondue

If using your own recipe, add a little extra blended cornflour (cornstarch) to the mixture as microwaved fondues tend to be thinner than those that are conventionally cooked. Do not keep fondues hot in the microwave, they will become stringy and curdled.

Cheese fondue ➤ *see Cheese, page 26*

French (green) beans

➤ *see Vegetables, pages 115–19*

Fries

➤ *see Chips, page 28*

Frosting

➤ *see Icing, page 58*

Frosting fruit

Suitable for small bunches of grapes, red, black or white currants for use as decoration for desserts. Lightly beat an egg white. Dip 6–8 bunches of fruit in the egg white, draining off any excess. Dip gently in caster (superfine) sugar, dusting the fruit all over until completely coated. Place in a circle on a sheet of non-stick baking parchment on a microwave rack (➤ *see page 75*) or a plate. Microwave on Medium-Low for 3–4 minutes until the frosting is dry and crisp, turning the fruit over after 1½ minutes.

Frozen meals

Frozen, ready-made meals have microwaving instructions on the packet. If there are no microwave instructions, it is unlikely that the meal should be microwaved, but this is usually clearly stated.

➤ *see also Labelling, page 63, and Plated Meals, page 84*

Fruit

Poaching fruit   Skin the fruit if liked (➤ *see overleaf*) or prick the skins to prevent bursting. Leave whole or cut into halves and remove any stones (pits). Arrange in a single layer in a casserole dish (Dutch oven). For 450 g/lb fruit, add 1 quantity of any of the sugar syrups on page 107, or use 300 ml/½ pt/¼ cups pure apple juice. Cover. Microwave on High for 3–8 minutes, turning the fruit over in the syrup once during cooking. Leave to stand for 2 minutes. Do not overcook or the fruit will disintegrate. *Peaches & plums if frozen are best on 50% for about 4 min, then 1–2 mins on 70%*

Stewing fruit   Peel, core, slice and remove stone (pits) as necessary. Place in an even layer in a casserole dish (Dutch oven). Sprinkle with sugar. Water is not necessary, but you can add up to 30 ml/2 tbsp water for extra juice. Cook for 2–10 minutes per 450 g/1 lb, depending on ripeness and type of fruit. As a rough guide, soft fruits take 2–5 minutes, hard fruits 6–10 minutes. Test and stir after 2 minutes, then after each further minute until cooked to your liking. Taste and add more sugar as necessary.

Skinning fresh fruit   Suitable for any soft fruit such as peaches, apricots, nectarines and tomatoes. Microwave each piece of fruit on High for 10–15 seconds. Leave to stand for 30 seconds, then peel off the skin.

Fruit, citrus

To get the most juice out of any citrus fruit, microwave on Medium-High for 30 seconds to 1 minute, until just warm, depending on the size of the fruit and the output of your microwave. Halve and squeeze as usual.

Fruit, dried

Dried fruit such as sultanas (golden raisins), raisins, currants or mixed dried fruit (fruit cake mix) can be easily plumped up for use in cakes and puddings. Place in a bowl and add any alcohol or juice from the recipe. Cover with a plate. Microwave on High until the fruit feels hot and has absorbed the liquid, checking and stirring every minute. Stir again and leave to stand until cold.

Dried fruit compôte   Put 225 g/8 oz any dried fruit (or a mixture such as dried fruit salad) in a bowl. Cover with 300 ml/½ pt/1¼ cups orange juice, cold tea or water. Flavour with a cinnamon stick, a clove or a few drops of vanilla essence (extract). Cover and microwave on High for 7–12 minutes until plump and soft, stirring once. Serve hot or leave to cool, then chill before serving.   *Mixture of fruit - soak - cook 6 min.*

Fruit, frozen   *Sugar makes skins hard - add later.*

Frozen fruits can be partially defrosted in the microwave, then left to finish thawing naturally.

Thawing free-flow, commercially frozen fruit   Leave to thaw naturally unless thawing and heating simultaneously.

Thawing fruit, home-frozen in dry sugar or syrup   Allow 2–4 minutes per 450 g/1 lb on High, then leave to thaw naturally.

Thawing fruit purée   Thaw as home-frozen fruit (➤ *see above*).

Fruit, glacé (candied)

Choose fresh fruit such as strawberries, orange, clementine or satsuma segments, grapes, cherries, lychees, kumquats, sliced peaches or nectarines, or pieces of pineapple, dried on kitchen paper (paper towels). You can also use suitable canned fruits but they must be drained and dried thoroughly on kitchen paper.

Put 100 g/4 oz granulated sugar and 75 ml/5 tbsp boiling water in a large measuring jug. Microwave on High for 1 minute, then stir. Whisk in

5 ml/1 tsp powdered glucose and microwave for 1 further minute. Stir until the sugar dissolves completely. Microwave on High for a further 5–7 minutes until the syrup is just beginning to turn golden – no more. Check frequently. Immediately stand the base of the jug in cold water to cool it quickly. Using a cocktail stick (toothpick), pierce a piece of fruit and dip in the syrup. Allow the excess to run off, then place on a piece of non-stick baking parchment to dry. Place in paper sweet cases (candy cups) before serving.

Fruit buns, thawing and warming

➤ *see Bread, page 16*

Fruits, fondant

➤ *see Icing, page 58*

Frying

It is not safe to shallow- or deep-fry in the microwave. However, there is a way to 'fry' eggs (➤ *see page 41*) and onions (➤ *see page 81*), and you can use a browning dish (➤ *see page 19*) to give similar results.

➤ *see also Stir-frying, page 105*

Fudge

Fudge is easily made in the microwave.

Chocolate fudge   Put 100 g/4 oz/½ cup butter or hard block margarine in a very large bowl and cut into pieces. Add 100 g/4 oz/1 cup plain (semi-sweet) chocolate, broken into pieces, 450 g/1 lb/2⅔ cups sifted icing (confectioners') sugar, 45 ml/3 tbsp milk and 5 ml/1 tsp vanilla essence (extract). Stir to mix a little. Cook on High for 2 minutes. Stir, then cook on High for a further 1–3 minutes until the chocolate and fat have melted. Beat well with a wooden spoon until thick and smooth. Turn into an oiled, shallow 18 × 28 cm/7 × 11 in tin (pan). Leave until cold, then chill until firm. Cut into small pieces and store in an airtight container.

White fudge   Make as Chocolate Fudge (above) but use white chocolate.

Full power

➤ *see High, page 56, and Power Output Settings, page 89*

G

Game

➣ see Poultry and Game, pages 86–8

Gammon

➣ see Meat, pages 71–4

Garlic bread

➣ see Bread, page 17

Gelatine

To use gelatine in a recipe, put the measured amount of powdered gelatine in a small bowl with 45–60 ml/3–4 tbsp liquid from the recipe. Leave to soften for 5 minutes. Place the bowl in the microwave and cook on High for 30 seconds. Stir, then cook in 10-second bursts for up to 30 seconds until completely dissolved. Do not allow to boil.

Glacé (candied) fruit

➣ see Fruit, Glacé, page 48

Glass

Ovenproof glass cookware is ideal for the microwave – but don't use your best crystal! You can also use glass jugs for warming milk, custard, etc.

➣ see also Dishes, page 37

Glazes

➣ see Bastes, page 12, Butter, page 22, and Coatings, page 32

Golden raisins

➣ see Fruit, Dried, page 48

Golden (light corn) syrup

Golden syrup is a good sweetener for cakes and puddings cooked in the microwave because it gives added colour.

Melting crystallised golden syrup   Syrup stored for a long time tends to crystallise. To make it liquid once more, remove the metal lid if in a jar, or if in a can, spoon into a bowl or jug. Microwave on Medium for 10–30 seconds until completely melted. Leave to cool before use.

Warm syrup sauce   Warm syrup makes a good sauce to pour over sponge puddings or pancakes. Spoon into a jug and microwave on Medium for 20–50 seconds or until runny but not boiling.

Gooseberries

> see Fruit, page 47

Granary bread, quick

> see Bread, page 17

Granola

This sweetened, crunchy high-grain cereal is expensive to buy but easy to make in the microwave.

Put 50 g/2 oz/¼ cup butter or margarine in a large bowl. Add 45 ml/ 3 tbsp golden (light corn) syrup. Microwave on Medium-Low for 2 minutes until melted. Stir in 150 g/5 oz/1¼ cups rolled oats, 20 g/ ¾ oz/scant ½ cup oat bran, 50 g/2 oz/¼ cup light brown sugar and 50 g/ 2 oz/½ cup chopped hazelnuts (filberts). Stir well. Microwave on High for 4–8 minutes, stirring frequently, until evenly browned. Stir in 40 g/ 1½ oz/¼ cup each of raisins and sultanas (golden raisins) and leave until cold and crisp. Store in an airtight container. Serve with milk to taste. Makes about 8 servings.

Grapefruit, grilled (broiled)

It is not possible to grill in a microwave, but this method gives similar results. Halve the grapefruit, place in individual dishes and separate the segments using a serrated edged knife in the usual way. Sprinkle with light brown sugar and add 5 ml/1 tsp sherry or orange liqueur to each, if liked. Place in the microwave and cook on High for about 1 minute per portion until the sugar is just melting. Leave to stand for 2 minutes before serving.

> see also Fruit, Citrus, page 48

Grapes, frosting

> see Frosting Fruit, page 47

Gravy

The gravy for the Sunday roast can be made in the microwave. Pour the meat juices into a measuring jug and make up to 300 ml/½ pt/1¼ cups with stock or vegetable cooking water. Mix 15–30 ml/1–2 tbsp cornflour (cornstarch) with a little water and stir in. Cook on High until bubbling and thickened, stirring after every minute. Add a little gravy browning if liked.

Reheating gravy   Pour into a serving jug. Microwave on Medium-High for 2–4 minutes until boiling, then stir and serve.

Greaseproof (waxed) paper

Use to cover foods to prevent spitting in the microwave. Also good for lining dishes to prevent sticking.
> ➤ *see also Covering Foods, page 33*

Greasing

It is not usually necessary to grease dishes when cooking in the microwave. The exceptions are when using a browning dish (➤ *see page 19*) and when making some puddings. If greasing is recommended, use oil or brush very sparingly with melted butter. Too much fat will impair the finished dish.

Green beans

> ➤ *see Vegetables, pages 115–19*

Greengages

> ➤ *see Fruit, page 47*

Grey mullet

> ➤ *see Fish, page 43*

Grilling (broiling)

Since this is not possible in a microwave, use your conventional grill (broiler) to brown and crisp foods after cooking in the microwave. Remember, the food is already cooked so it will only take a few minutes.
➤ *see also Browning Dish, page 19, and Browning Element, page 21*

Ground meat

> ➤ *see Meat, page 71*

Grouse

> ➤ *see Poultry and Game, pages 86–8*

Guinea fowl

> ➤ *see Poultry and Game, pages 86–8*

Haddock

> see Fish, page 43

Hake

> see Fish, page 43

Ham

> see Meat, pages 71–4

Hamburgers

> see Burgers, page 21

Hare

> see Poultry and Game, pages 86–8

Haricot (navy) beans

> see Pulses, page 90

Hazelnuts (filberts)

> see Nuts, page 79

Herbs, drying

Wash sprigs of fresh herbs and dry on kitchen paper (paper towels). Do not remove the stalks. Lay them in a single layer on a sheet of kitchen paper on a large plate or straight in the microwave. Put a small cup of water beside the herbs to absorb some of the energy. Microwave on High until the herbs lose their bright colour and will crumble easily. Check every 30 seconds and rearrange the sprigs every minute. Leave until cold, then crumble into an airtight container, discarding the stalks. Store in a cool, dark place.

Note: Chives are best snipped into small pieces before drying.

Herrings

> see Fish, page 44

Herrings, soused

> see Fish, page 44

High

This is the maximum power output of your microwave, also known as Full Power or 100 per cent wattage. It is used for most general cooking purposes.

> ➤ *see also Power Output Settings, page 89*

Hollandaise sauce

> ➤ *see Sauces, Egg-based, page 98*

Honey

Honey makes a good sweetening agent instead of white sugar or golden (light corn) syrup. Honey that has crystallised can be made liquid again by melting in the microwave. Remove the metal lid from the jar, place in the oven and heat on Medium for 10–30 seconds. Leave to cool before using.

Honey and lemon drink   Soothing when you have a cold or sore throat. Put 30 ml/2 tbsp clear honey in a mug with the juice of 1 small lemon. Top up with water. Microwave on High for 1–2 minutes until comfortably warm. Stir well and sip. Stir in a little more honey, if liked.

Hot and cold spots

Most microwave ovens do not cook completely evenly. There are often hot or cold spots where the food either cooks more quickly or takes longer to cook. Many ovens have a turntable, others have stirrer paddles in the base of the oven to help to rectify this, but it important to turn and rearrange foods during cooking to ensure even heating.

Hot dogs

Prick 4 hot dog sausages and place in finger rolls. Wrap individually in kitchen paper (paper towels) and microwave on High for 1–3 minutes, rearranging once. Open and serve in the kitchen paper, with mustard and ketchup (catsup). Add fried onions (➤ *see page 81*), if liked.

Huss

> ➤ *see Fish, page 43*

I

Ice cream

Put 300 ml/½ pt/1¼ cups milk in a measuring jug. Microwave on High for 1½–3 minutes, stirring once, until hot but not boiling. Whisk 100 g/4 oz/ ½ cup caster (superfine) sugar with 2 eggs, 10 ml/2 tsp cornflour (cornstarch) and 5 ml/1 tsp vanilla essence (extract) until thick and pale. Pour on the hot milk, whisking all the time. Microwave on High for 2–4 minutes, whisking after every minute until thickened and smooth. Leave to cool. Fold in 300 ml/½ pt/1¼ cups whipped cream (I use a low-fat variety). Turn into a freezerproof container and freeze for 2 hours until frozen round the edges. Whisk well with a fork to break up the ice crystals. Freeze again until firm. Makes 4–6 servings.

Cassata   Make Ice Cream as above and fold in 100 g/4 oz/1 cup chopped glacé (candied) fruit after whisking to break up the ice crystals.

Chocolate chip ice cream   Make Ice Cream as above. Stir in 50 g/2 oz/ ½ cup chocolate chips after whisking to break up the ice crystals.

Mint chocolate chip ice cream   Make as for Chocolate Chip Ice Cream but use peppermint essence (extract) instead of vanilla, to taste, and add a few drops of green food colouring, if liked.

Coffee ice cream   Make Ice Cream as above and dissolve 15 ml/1 tbsp instant coffee powder with the milk.

Rum and raisin ice cream   Put 50 g/2 oz/⅓ cup raisins and 30 ml/2 tbsp rum in a small bowl. Cover with a saucer and microwave on High for 1½–2 minutes or until the fruit has absorbed the liquid. Leave to cool. Stir into Ice Cream (➤ *see above*) after whisking to break up the ice crystals.

To loosen an ice cream bombe for turning out   Place in the microwave and cook on Medium-Low for 20–30 seconds, then turn out.

To soften ice cream   Put a 1 litre/1¾ pt/4¼ cup block or tub of hard ice cream in the microwave and loosen the lid. Microwave on Medium-Low for 1½–2 minutes. Leave to stand for 2 minutes before serving.
   Note: This is not suitable for soft-scoop!

Icing (frosting)

Chocolate fudge icing   Cut up 100 g/4 oz/½ cup butter and put in a bowl. Cover with a sheet of kitchen paper (paper towel) and microwave on High for 1 minute. Stir until completely melted. Sift 350 g/12 oz/2 cups icing (confectioners') sugar, 20 g/¾ oz/3 tbsp cocoa powder and 5 ml/1 tsp instant coffee powder together. Gradually beat into the butter until thick and well blended. The mixture will appear grainy. Leave to stand until it reaches a stiff, spreadable consistency. Makes enough to cover the top and sides of a 20 cm/8 in round cake.

Drying icing   Royal icing lattice shapes or flowers may be dried in the microwave. Place on greaseproof (waxed) paper on a board or plate and microwave on Medium-Low for 10–15 seconds. Leave to stand for 3 minutes, then repeat until dry. Don't use longer bursts or the icing may scorch.

Fondant icing   Bought fondant icing that is too hard to use may be softened or melted in the microwave.

To soften, remove foil wrapper; place on kitchen paper (paper towels) in the microwave. Heat on Medium-Low for 1–1½ minutes. Knead gently.

To melt, cut the block into chunks. Place in a bowl and microwave on Medium-High for 2–2½ minutes, stirring every 30 seconds until melted. Do not continue to cook once the mixture is runny. Use while still warm for piping writing on cakes or to dip soft fruits in to serve with coffee after dinner (➤ *see below*). The icing will harden as it cools.

Making fondant fruits   Use strawberries with their hulls on, physalis with the papery leaves folded back, cherries on their stalks or grapes with a tiny stalk left on. Hold each fruit by the stalk. Dip in the melted fondant (➤ *see above*), then leave to dry on non-stick baking parchment. Place in paper sweet cases (candy cups) before serving.

Insulating food

➤ *see Standing Time, page 104*

Ironstone pottery

This is not suitable for cooking in the microwave as it absorbs microwaves, and becomes hot.

Jam (conserve)

Making jam in the microwave is clean and efficient. You can use your normal recipes. For best results, follow these general rules:

- Do not make more than 1.8 kg/4 lb jam in one go.
- Sterilise the jars (> *see Sterilising, page 105*).
- Warm the preserving sugar before use. It will take 2–3 minutes on Medium to warm 450 g/1 lb.
- Use a very large bowl to prevent boiling over – for 900 g/2 lb fruit use a 3.25 litre/6 pt/15 cup bowl or one with at least three times the capacity of the ingredients.
- Dissolve the warmed sugar completely in the fruit before starting to boil the mixture to make it set. Stir and test (> *see below*) after every minute to see if it sets.
- Do not use a conventional sugar thermometer. Test by putting a small spoonful of the mixture on a cold saucer. Push your finger through the jam. If the surface wrinkles, the mixture is ready to set.
- Use oven gloves to remove the bowl from the oven as it will be VERY hot.
- Pot, cover and label in your usual way.

Jam sauce Heat equal quantities of jam and water in a jug on High, stirring once or twice until melted and hot. Spike with a squeeze of lemon juice, if liked. Serve with sponge puddings or over fruit with ice cream.

Jelly (jello)

To dissolve jelly cubes Break up the tablet and place the cubes in a measuring jug. Make up to 300 ml/½ pt/1¼ cups with water. Microwave on High for 1–2½ minutes until dissolved, stirring once. Stir in ice cubes or cold water to make up to 600 ml/1 pt/2½ cups, pour into a serving dish or mould, leave until cold, then chill until set. Turn out, if desired, and serve.

To loosen set jelly in a glass or plastic mould for turning out Place the mould in the microwave and microwave on Medium for 10–20 seconds. Gently pull the jelly from the sides of the mould, then invert on a plate, shake firmly and remove the mould.

Note: Do not use this method to loosen a metal mould.

Jerusalem artichokes

> *see Vegetables, pages 115–19*

Puréed Jerusalem artichokes Cook the artichokes according to the instructions on page 116. Drain and turn into a blender or food processor. Add a knob of butter or margarine, a good pinch of grated nutmeg and a generous grinding of black pepper. Run the machine until the vegetables are smooth. Serve with game, or thin with milk or stock, reheat for 2–4 minutes on High and serve as a soup.

K

Kebabs

Because kebabs are made with tender cuts of meat, fish, offal or poultry, they cook well in a microwave. For best results, follow these general rules:

- Marinate meat or poultry first for added flavour and colour (➤ *see Marinades, page 69*).
- Cut foods into even-sized pieces for more even cooking.
- Use soaked wooden skewers, not metal ones, and cook up to four at one time.
- Place on a microwave rack (➤ *see page 75*) over a plate to catch any juices, or use a browning dish (➤ *see page 19*).
- Cover with a dome of greaseproof (waxed) paper to prevent splattering.
- Microwave on High for 1–2 minutes per kebab, then turn over. Continue cooking in 30-second bursts, turning again if necessary, until cooked to your liking (the exact time depends on the foods and quantity used).
- Baste with the marinade or juices on the plate during cooking.

Kidney beans

➤ *see Pulses, page 90*

Kidneys

Kidneys cook quickly so care should be taken. They are best cooked in liquid. Cut or slice 8 kidneys, removing the cores. Place in a dish and add 300 ml/½ pt/1¼ cups chicken, beef, lamb or vegetable stock, or use a 295 g/10½ oz/medium can of condensed mushroom, tomato or celery soup. Add a pinch of dried basil, mixed herbs or oregano. Cover and cook on High until the liquid boils. Turn down to Medium and cook, stirring every minute, until the kidneys are tender. Do not overcook. If cooked in stock, blend 30 ml/2 tbsp cornflour (cornstarch) with a little water in a bowl. Strain the kidneys and add the stock to the bowl. Stir well. Microwave on High for 2 minutes, stirring once, until thickened and smooth. Season to taste and stir in a little crème fraîche, if liked. Serve with rice (➤ *see page 94*) or pasta (➤ *see page 82*). Serves 4.

Kippers

➤ *see Fish, page 43, and Boil-in-the-bag Packs, page 14*

Kitchen paper (paper towels)

Kitchen paper can be used to stop splattering and to absorb moisture in the microwave during cooking.

➤ *see also Covering Foods, page 33*

Kohl rabi

Cook as for turnips (➤ *see Vegetables, page 117*).

Labelling

* Reproduced courtesy of the Ministry of Agriculture, Fisheries and Food

Most new domestic microwave ovens now display a label which ties in with the labels on food packs referring to microwave cooking. Matching the information on the food pack with that on the oven will give the heating time needed. The oven label, an example of which is given below, shows three important pieces of information.

the microwave symbol

the power output (watts)

the heating category for small packs

The microwave symbol

The symbol below shows that the oven has been labelled in compliance with the new scheme.

The power output

The figure in the box below shows the power output of the oven, in watts, based on an internally agreed standard (IEC 705).

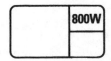

If your oven is rated 700 watt it will heat faster than a 600 watt oven, but not as fast as a 800/850 watt or a 900/1000 watt oven (➤ *see below*).

o v e n   p o w e r   r a t i n g

500W	600W	700W	800W

◀ more heating time   less heating time ▶

The heating category
In this box there will be a letter denoting your oven's heating category. It is based on the oven's ability to heat small food packs. Instructions on food packs up to 500 g are likely to be given in terms of these letters (➤ *see below*).

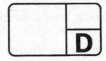

If your oven category is C it will heat up small portions of food faster than category A or B but not as fast as category D or E ovens (➤ *see below*).

heating category for small packs

A	B	C	D	E

◀ more heating time   less heating time ▶

The food pack label
Most packaged food suitable for microwaving will be marked with the microwave symbol and appropriate instructions for heating. Below is an illustration of the type of label used.

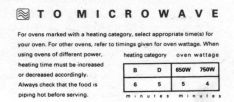

≋ **T O   M I C R O W A V E**

For ovens marked with a heating category, select appropriate time(s) for your oven. For other ovens, refer to timings given for oven wattage. When using ovens of different power, heating time must be increased or decreased accordingly. Always check that the food is piping hot before serving.

heating category		oven wattage	
B	D	650W	750W
6	5	5	4
minutes		minutes	

Using heating category instructions
In the illustration above, the information given is for B and D ovens only. For C ovens, choose the time midway between B and D, in this case 5½ minutes. For A ovens, it will be necessary to heat food for a little longer than the time given for B ovens, in this case 6½ minutes. For E ovens, use a slightly shorter heating time than that specified for D ovens, in this case 4½ minutes. After heating, always check that the food is piping hot throughout.

Using oven wattage instructions
The illustration also gives information for 650 watt and 750 watt ovens.

For ovens with a wattage lower than 650 watts, heat for a slightly longer time, approximately 6 minutes for a 500–600 watt cooker. For ovens with a wattage higher than 750 watts, you will need a slightly shorter time, approximately 3 minutes for 800–850 watts and 2½ minutes for 900–1000 watts.

After heating, always check food is piping hot throughout. If not, heat a little longer.

Foodline If you need further help to understand the instructions on food packs, a free helpline is available through the Food Safety Advisory Centre to offer practical advice. Freephone: 0207 808 7256.

Ladies' fingers

➤ *see Vegetables, pages 115–19*

Lamb

➤ *see Meat, pages 71–4*

Lasagne

Make a Bolognese Sauce (➤ *see page 15*). Make a Cheese Sauce (➤ *see page 98*). Layer the Bolognese Sauce with sheets of no-need-to-precook lasagne in a fairly shallow, flameproof dish. Pour the Cheese Sauce over. Cook on High for 10–15 minutes until the lasagne feels tender when a knife is inserted down through the centre. Place the dish under a hot grill (broiler) for a few minutes to lightly brown the top, if liked. If not, leave to stand for 5 minutes before serving. Serves 4.

Leeks

Put the tomatos under the lasagne so it doesn't stick to the dish.

➤ *see Vegetables, pages 115–19*

Lemon curd

➤ *see Curds, page 36*

Lemon meringue pie

Make and cook a pastry case (pie shell), ➤ *see page 83*. Make up a packet of lemon meringue pie filling in the usual way but substitute lemon juice for 15 ml/1 tbsp of the water. Spoon into the cooked pastry case. Make up the conventional meringue topping, using 1 egg white and 50 g/2 oz/¼ cup caster (superfine) sugar. Pile on the pie. Sprinkle with light brown sugar and microwave on High for 1½–2½ minutes until set. It will be a soft, not crisp, meringue.

Lemonade

Scrub 3 large lemons, cut into halves and squeeze the juice. Pour into a large bowl. Add the lemon shells, 100 g/4 oz/½ cup granulated sugar and 300 ml/½ pt/1¼ cups water. Microwave on High for 2–3 minutes. Stir well until the sugar completely dissolves. Microwave on High for a further 1–2 minutes until boiling. Remove from the microwave and leave until cold. Strain into a jug and stir in 150 ml/¼ pt/⅔ cup water. Chill until ready to serve, poured over lots of ice.

Lemons

➤ *see Fruit, Citrus, page 48, and Zest, page 125*

Lentils

➤ *see Pulses, page 90*

Light corn syrup

➤ *see Golden Syrup, page 51*

Lime curd

➤ *see Curds, page 36*

Limes

➤ *see Fruit, Citrus, page 48, and Zest, page 125*

Lining containers

Non-stick baking parchment or greaseproof (waxed) paper can be used to line the base of containers where food is to be turned out e.g. cakes or puddings. There is no need to grease the container in most cases.

➤ *see also Greasing, page 53, and Cakes, Sponge, page 23*

Liver

Slice and cook as for kidneys (➤ *see page 61*) or use a browning dish (➤ *see page 19*).

Liver pâté

Pâtés and terrines cook much more quickly in a microwave. Prepare in your normal way. Turn into a suitable container. Cover with greaseproof (waxed) paper. Cook on Medium-High for 20–30 minutes per 900 g/2 lb meat until the mixture feels just firm to the touch. Cover with clean greaseproof paper and weigh down with heavy weights. Leave until cold, then chill overnight.

Low

This is the minimum power output of your microwave, 10 per cent of the total wattage. Use for keeping foods warm, infusing sauces and some thawing.

> ➤ *see also Power Output Settings, page 89*

Low-fat spreads

Use as butter (➤ *see page 22*).

Macaroni cheese

Put 175 g/6 oz short-cut macaroni in a large dish with 900 ml/1½ pts/ 3¾ cups boiling water. Cook on High for 6–8 minutes, stirring twice until just tender. Leave to stand while preparing the rest of the dish. Put 40 g/ 1½ oz/⅓ cup plain (all-purpose) flour in a bowl. Whisk in 450 ml/¾ pt/ 3 cups milk. Add a good knob of butter or margarine. Microwave on High for 4–6 minutes, whisking after every minute until thick and smooth. Stir in 75 g/3 oz/¾ cup grated Cheddar cheese, 2.5 ml/½ tsp English mustard and a little salt and freshly ground black pepper. Drain the macaroni and stir into the sauce. Turn into a flameproof serving dish. Sprinkle with 25 g/1 oz/¼ cup grated cheese and a handful of crushed cornflakes. Place under a hot grill (broiler) to brown. Serves 4.

Mackerel

➤ see Fish, page 43

Mackerel, soused

➤ see Fish, page 44

Magnetron

The magnetron is situated in the top of your microwave cooker. It converts everyday electricity into microwaves.

Mangetout (snow peas)

➤ see Vegetables, pages 115–19

Margarine

➤ see Butter, page 22

Marinades

Steep meat, poultry or game in a marinade for several hours or overnight to add flavour and colour and to tenderise meats before their quick-cooking in the microwave. The following quantities will marinate 450 g/ 1 lb meat.

Wine marinade   Mix 45 ml/3 tbsp red or white wine with the same quantity of olive or sunflower oil. Add 2.5 ml/½ tsp dried herbs of your choice (I like sage or oregano for pork, rosemary, mint or oregano for lamb, sage or thyme for poultry and basil or mixed herbs for beef). Whisk in 5 ml/1 tsp dried onion or garlic granules, a good grinding of black pepper and 5 ml/1 tsp Worcestershire or soy sauce.

Balsamic sherry marinade   Mix 45 ml/3 tbsp olive or sunflower oil with 15 ml/1 tbsp balsamic vinegar, 15 ml/1 tbsp medium sherry, 10 ml/2 tsp soy sauce and 5 ml/1 tsp garlic granules (or a crushed fresh clove).

Barbecue marinade   Whisk together 30 ml/2 tbsp olive or sunflower oil with 15 ml/1 tbsp tomato ketchup (catsup), 15 ml/1 tbsp Worcestershire sauce, 15 ml/1 tbsp golden (light corn) syrup, 10 ml/2 tsp malt vinegar and 10 ml/2 tsp soy sauce.

Marjoram

➤ *see Herbs, Drying, page 55*

Marmalade

Follow all the rules for jam (conserve), ➤ *see page 59*, and don't try to make more than 1.8 kg/4 lbs marmalade in one go. The fruit is prepared in your normal way but you will need to soften the peel before continuing with the marmalade recipe. Place the shredded or finely chopped peel in a bowl with 150 ml/¼ pt/⅔ cup water (taken from the total amount required). Cover with a plate and microwave on High for 5–8 minutes until soft. Now continue with the recipe, adding the peel and any liquid to the remaining ingredients. Lightly crush the pips, tie in a piece of muslin (or an unused piece of disposable dish cloth) and add to the bowl of marmalade as it cooks to release its pectin and help setting. Test for setting as for jam.

Marrow (squash)

➤ *see Vegetables, pages 115–19*

Stuffed marrow   Prepare either the Bolognese Sauce mixture (➤ *see page 15*) or Chilli Con Carne (➤ *see page 27*). Boil for a few minutes extra to reduce the liquid content. Arrange peeled and seeded rings of marrow in a large, shallow dish. Spoon the meat mixture into the centre of each. Cover with a lid or dome of greaseproof (waxed) paper and microwave on High for 6–10 minutes. Turn the rings gently after 4 minutes. The marrow should feel just soft when pierced with a knife. Leave to stand for 3 minutes before serving. Serves 4.

Marzipan

To soften marzipan   Remove any foil wrapper from a 250 g/9 oz block. Place on a piece of kitchen paper (paper towel). Microwave on Medium-Low for 1–2 minutes. Knead gently and use as required.

Meat

For best results when cooking meat, follow these general rules:

- Position meat with the thickest parts towards the outside. Protect thin parts or bone ends with thin strip of smooth foil (➤ *see Shielding, page 101*).
- Thaw meat completely before cooking (➤ *see Meat Thawing Times, page 73*).
- Usually, if meat takes more than 15 minutes to cook, it will brown naturally because of the high fat content. However, it won't look as brown as when cooked conventionally, so use a browning agent (➤ *see page 18*), or marinade (➤ *see page 69*) or place in a roaster bag (➤ *see Covering Foods, page 33*) to assist the process.
- When using a roaster bag, put the meat on a microwave rack (➤ *see page 75*) or upturned saucer over a plate and make a small slit in the base of the bag so the juices drain on to the plate.
- Don't salt meat before cooking or it will toughen the surface.
- Never use a conventional meat thermometer in the microwave, use a specific microwave thermometer (➤ *see page 74*).
- For kebabs, use soaked wooden skewers, not metal.
- If using a browning dish for more than one batch of food, reheat for half the original time before re-using (➤ *see Browning Dish, page 19*).
- Meat is best cooked from room temperature. If cooking straight from the fridge, add a further 1–2 minutes per 450 g/1 lb.

Cooking times Meat roasted in the microwave is not, in my opinion, as good as that cooked conventionally. The chart overleaf gives you complete cooking times. However, ideally I recommend a combination of the two methods which will substantially reduce cooking times and save fuel. Weigh your joint and cook for half its cooking time (calculated by weight) in the microwave, then transfer to a hot conventional oven for the remaining cooking time (by weight). For example, a 1.75 kg/4 lb leg of lamb should be cooked in the microwave for 12–16 minutes, then transferred to a hot conventional oven for 40 minutes. This saves about an hour. (While the meat is microwaving, get your potatoes in the top of the oven to start roasting.)

Meat cooking times

Type of meat	Preparation	Roasting time per 450 g/ 1 lb on Medium-High	Standing time
Beef joint	Place on a microwave rack over a plate. Cover with a roaster bag. Turn halfway through cooking.	Rare: 6–8 minutes Medium: 8–10 minutes Well done: 9–12 minutes	Cover with a dome of foil. Stand for 15–20 minutes, for rare; 20–25 minutes, for medium/well done.
Beef steaks	Use a browning dish (*see page 19*) or cook conventionally.		
Lamb joints, on the bone	Prepare as for beef joints. Cover bone end with a thin strip of foil.	Medium: 6–8 minutes Well done: 9–12 minutes	Cover with a dome of foil. Stand for 20–25 minutes.
Lamb joints, boned	Stuff, if liked. Weigh after stuffing. Prepare as for beef joints.	Medium: 7–9 minutes Well done: 10–12 minutes	Cover with a dome of foil. Stand for 30 minutes.
Lamb chops	Add a browning agent (*see page 18*). Arrange in a circle on a microwave rack, bones inward. Cover with a roaster bag.	4 chops: 5–8 minutes, turning once.	Cover with foil, leave to stand for 2 minutes.
Pork joint, on the bone	Prepare as for beef joints.	7–10 minutes, turning once.	Cover with a dome of foil. Stand for 30 minutes.
Pork joint, boned	Stuff, if liked. Prepare as for boned lamb.	8–12 minutes, turning once.	As above.
Pork chops	Prepare as for lamb chops.	4 chops: 8–10 minutes, depending on thickness, turning once.	As for lamb chops.
Gammon/ ham joint	Prepare as for beef joints, place in a casserole dish (Dutch oven) and add 150 ml/ ¼ pt/⅔ cup cider.	9–12 minutes, turning once.	Cover with a dome of foil. Stand for 30 minutes.
Gammon steaks	Place on a microwave rack, cover with a roaster bag (*see page 33*).	2 medium steaks: 3–6 minutes, turning once.	Cover with foil, stand for 2 minutes.
Veal joint, on the bone	Prepare as for beef joints. Protect bone end with thin strip of foil.	6–9 minutes, turning once.	Cover with a dome of foil. Stand for 30 minutes.
Veal joint, boned	Stuff if liked. Prepare as for beef joints.	7–10 minutes.	As above.
Veal chops	Prepare as for lamb chops.	2 chops: 3–6 minutes, turning once.	Cover with foil. Stand for 2 minutes.

Meat temperature chart The meat should always feel tender when tested with a skewer, but the temperature is a more accurate test to check the joint is cooked to your liking. Use a meat thermometer or a microwave probe or thermometer (➤ *see page 74*) and the chart below.

Type of meat	Remove from the microwave when	Temperature after standing	Approximate cooking time per 450 g/1 lb on Medium-High
Beef, rare	49°C/120°F	60°C/140°F	6–8 minutes
Beef, medium	60°C/140°F	71°C/160°F	8–10 minutes
Beef, well done	71°C/160°F	77°C/170°F	10–12 minutes
Lamb, medium	66°C/150°F	77°C/170°F	7–9 minutes
Lamb, well done	71°C/160°F	82°C/180°F	10–12 minutes
Pork/gammon/ham	82°C/180°F	88°C/190°F	8–12 minutes
Veal	66°C/150°F	77°C/170°F	6–10 minutes
Chicken	82°C/180°F	88°C/190°F	7–10 minutes
Turkey	79°C/175°F	90°C/195°F	8–11 minutes

Meat thawing times Use the chart below to calculate the time required to thaw meat.

Cut of meat	Preparation	Thawing time per 450 g/1 lb at Medium-Low	Standing time
Joint with bone	Place on a plate, cover loosely with greaseproof (waxed) paper.	5–8 minutes	Wrap in foil and stand for 30 minutes halfway through microwaving. Finish thawing naturally.
Joint without bone	As above.	8–10 minutes	As above.
Steaks and chops	As above. Put thickest parts facing out.	6–10 minutes (depending on thickness)	Wrap in foil and stand for 5–10 minutes to finish thawing.
Diced stewing meat	As above, break up as soon as possible and move frozen pieces to outside.	8 minutes	Wrap in foil, and stand for 10–12 minutes to finish thawing.
Offal (liver, kidneys, etc.)	As above, separate as soon as possible.	8 minutes	Wrap in foil, and stand for 5 minutes to finish thawing.
Bacon rashers (slices)	Leave in plastic vacuum wrap, but pierce the wrap, or as above. Separate as soon as possible and remove as soon as thawed.	6 minutes	No standing time necessary.

Cut of meat	Preparation	Thawing time per 450 g/1 lb at Medium-Low	Standing time
Sausages	Leave in wrapper. Open and separate as soon as possible.	8 minutes *5 min* 30%	Wrap in foil, leave to stand for 5 minutes to finish thawing.
Minced (ground) meat	As above. Scrape off meat as it thaws and place in a bowl.	8 minutes	No extra standing time necessary.

Meat thermometer

➤ *see Microwave Thermometer, page 75*

Medium

This setting is equivalent to 50 per cent of the total wattage of your microwave. Use when slower cooking is required, for more delicate foods.

➤ *see also Power Output Settings, page 89*

Medium-High

This setting uses 70 per cent of the total wattage of your microwave, good for roasting meats and cooking cakes. Particularly useful on very high wattage cookers when 100 per cent power can be too fierce.

➤ *see also Power Output Settings, page 89*

Medium-Low

Equivalent to 30 per cent of the total wattage of your microwave. Particularly useful for thawing foods or melting butter or chocolate.

➤ *see also Power Output Settings, page 89*

Meringues

Micro-meringues are pure white and crisp. They take very little time or fuel and 1 egg white goes a long way. The downside is you have to use an enormous amount of sugar!

Whisk 1 egg white until frothy but not stiff. Gradually beat in 350 g/ 12 oz/2 cups sifted icing (confectioners') sugar. When the mixture becomes stiff, knead in the remaining sugar until the mixture forms a stiff paste. Cut in half and roll out each half to a sausage shape. Cut each sausage into 24 pieces and roll into balls. Place six in a circle on a sheet on non-stick baking parchment on a plate. Microwave on High for 1¼–2½ minutes until crisp and dry. Remove from the microwave, leave to stand for 5 minutes, then transfer to a wire rack to cool completely. Repeat with the remaining batches of meringues. Store in an airtight container. Serve with desserts or sandwich together in pairs with cream.

Pavlova   Prepare the meringue mixture (➤ *see page 74*). Divide in half and roll each half into an 18 cm/7 in round. Hollow the centre slightly. Microwave on High for 2 minutes. Leave to stand for 1 minute, then microwave again for 2 minutes until crisp and dry. Leave to stand for 5 minutes, then transfer to a wire rack to cool. Repeat with the remaining half. Top with cream and fruit when cold. Serves 4.

Vacherin   Prepare the meringue mixture (➤ *see page 74*). Cut in half and roll out each half to an 18 cm/7 in round. Place on a sheet of non-stick baking parchment on a plate. Microwave on High for 2 minutes. Leave to stand for 1 minute. Microwave again for a further 2 minutes or until crisp and dry. Leave to stand for 5 minutes, then transfer to a wire rack to cool completely. Repeat with the remaining meringue. When cold, sandwich together with whipped cream and fresh fruit. Drizzle the top with melted chocolate (➤ *see Chocolate, page 28*). Serves 4.

Meringue pies

➤ *see Lemon Meringue Pie, page 65*

Microwave labelling

➤ *see Labelling, page 63*

Microwave output

➤ *see Cooking Times, page 31, and Power Output Settings, page 89*

Microwave rack

A microwave rack is a specially coated rack with feet that is placed in the oven. During the cooking process, air and microwaves can circulate more freely around the food on the rack and juices or other liquids can drain away.

Microwave settings

➤ *see Power Output Settings, page 89*

Microwave thermometer

This is specially designed to be inserted in the meat or poultry and used while the microwave is on. A conventional meat thermometer should only be inserted once the meat is removed from the oven. Some microwaves have a probe attached to the oven cavity. It is inserted into the meat and the cooker will switch off automatically when the meat reaches the correct temperature. The temperature of the meat will rise on standing as it completes cooking.

Microwaves

Microwaves are similar to radio waves. In a conventional cooker, heat is radiated round the food. It starts cooking the outside, then gradually penetrates the food until it is cooked through, giving the traditional brown, cooked appearance to the surface. But in a microwave oven, the microwaves pass into the food to a depth of about 5 cm/2 in. These waves make the water molecules in the food vibrate. This generates the heat which cooks the food. Because there is no outside source of heat, the food does not become brown or crisp on the surface.

Milk

To warm milk for drinking or pouring on cereals, pour into a cup or jug. Microwave on High for 1–2 minutes per 200 ml/7 fl oz/scant 1 cup. Stir before use.

Milk puddings

Creamy rice, semolina (cream of wheat), tapioca or sago can be made in the microwave. For best results follow these general rules:
- Use a very large dish to prevent boiling over.
- Put your usual quantity of rice, semolina, etc. in the container with the sugar and milk and stir well.
- Cook on High until the milk boils. Stir again.
- Turn down to Medium and continue cooking for 10–40 minutes (depending on the grain) or until the mixture is creamy and the grains are soft, stirring two or three times. The longer you cook, the creamer it will be.

➤ *see also Rice Pudding, page 95*

Milk-based sauces

➤ *see Sauces, Milk-based, page 98*

Minced (ground) meat

➤ *see Meat, pages 71–4, and individual recipes*

Mince pies

Mince pies cannot be cooked successfully in the microwave but they can be reheated. Arrange in a circle on a plate (removing any foil containers). Heat on Medium for about 20 seconds per pie. Heat just until the pastry (paste) feels warm. Do not overheat or the filling will be burning hot and the pastry soft.

Mint

> see Herbs, Drying, page 55

Mint chocolate chip ice cream

> see Ice Cream, page 57

Moules marinière

> see Fish, page 44

Moussaka

Chop an onion. Place in a large bowl with 350 g/12 oz minced (ground) beef or lamb. Cook on High for 4–5 minutes, stirring twice, until the meat is no longer pink and all the grains are separate. Stir in 2.5 ml/½ tsp each of ground cinnamon and dried oregano, 150 ml/¼ pt/⅔ cup beef or lamb stock made with ½ stock cube and 30 ml/2 tbsp tomato purée (paste). Cook on High for 3–5 minutes, stirring once. Season to taste and add a pinch of caster (superfine) sugar. Scrub and thinly slice 450 g/1 lb potatoes. Place in a shallow dish and add 30 ml/2 tbsp water. Cover and cook on High for 4–6 minutes until just tender, stirring once. Drain. Layer the meat and potatoes in a dish, finishing with a layer of potatoes. Beat an egg with 150 ml/¼ pt/⅔ cup plain yoghurt and a little salt and freshly ground black pepper. Pour over. Microwave on High for 7–10 minutes until piping hot and the top is set. The moussaka should feel tender when a knife is inserted down through the centre. Sprinkle with 30 ml/2 tbsp grated Cheddar cheese and brown under a hot grill (broiler). Serves 4.

with all ingredients cooked, put layers in a dish & pour over the egg mixture. 12 min. on High.

Mousses

To release a mousse from its mould, put the set mousse in the microwave. Cook on Medium-Low for 20–40 seconds. Then invert on a serving plate and remove the mould.

Note: This method should not be used for metal moulds.

When thawing mousse, don't try to thaw it completely. Microwave on Medium-Low for 2–3 minutes only, then leave to stand to thaw naturally.

Mulled wine

Pour a bottle of red wine in a large bowl. Stir in 30 ml/2 tbsp caster (superfine) sugar, 30 ml/2 tbsp brandy, a few slices of orange and lemon, a 5 cm/2 in piece of cinnamon stick and 2 cloves. Microwave on Medium for 3–5 minutes until very hot but not boiling, stirring twice. Serve hot.

Mullet, grey or red

> *see Fish, page 43*

Mung beans

> *see Pulses, page 90*

Mushrooms

Mushrooms need no extra water when cooking in the microwave. Wash 100 g/4 oz even-sized mushrooms. Place in a bowl. Cover with a plate and microwave on High for 2–3 minutes. Stir, then leave to stand for 2 minutes before serving.

Garlic mushrooms Wash 225 g/8 oz button mushrooms. Place in a bowl with 25 g/1 oz/2 tbsp butter or margarine, 1–2 crushed garlic cloves and 30 ml/2 tbsp chopped parsley. Add a good grinding of black pepper. Cover with a plate and cook on High for 2–3 minutes. Stir, re-cover and cook for a further 2–3 minutes until cooked through and bathed in buttery juices. Leave to stand for 2 minutes, then spoon on to plates and serve with hot bread. Serves 4. *stuffed mushrooms (big) take 7 mins.*

Mussels

> *see Fish, page 44*

To thaw cooked frozen mushrooms: use veg. pot, empty 1 small packet into it, power 1 min, 100°

Napkins

Cotton and linen napkins can be used to wrap bread rolls in for warming in the microwave (➢ *see Bread, page 17*). Don't use napkins made of synthetic fibres.

Navy beans

➢ *see Pulses, page 90*

Nectarines

➢ *see Fruit, page 47*

Non-stick baking parchment

This can be used to line the bases of containers when cooking cakes or some puddings. No greasing is required.

➢ *See also Covering Foods, page 33, Lining Containers, page 66, and Greasing, page 53*

Nuts

A microwave is extremely useful for skinning and shelling nuts and for preparing delicious crunchy snacks. Nuts also make a good topping for sweet and savoury dishes to enhance the colour and texture.

Blanching almonds   Place 100 g/4 oz/1 cup nuts with their skins on in a bowl and add 150 ml/¼ pt/⅔ cup water. Microwave on High for 1½ –2½ minutes. Drain and when cool enough to handle, slip off the skins between the finger and thumb.

Cooking chestnuts   Make a slit in the skins with a sharp knife to prevent them bursting. Place in a shallow bowl in an even layer. Cook on Medium-High for 3–6 minutes, checking every minute and removing the nuts as they soften. Peel off the skins while still hot (using gloves or a cloth). Do not overcook or they will harden.

Dry-roasting whole nuts   Spread the nuts out on a piece of kitchen paper (paper towel) in a shallow dish. Do not add any oil. Microwave on High for 3–5 minutes, tossing after every minute, until browned. Leave until cold, then store in an airtight container.

Roasting whole nuts   Place 100 g/4 oz/1 cup raw, shelled nuts in a shallow dish. Stir in 15 ml/1 tbsp sunflower or peanut (groundnut) oil and spread out evenly. Microwave on High for 3–5 minutes, stirring after every minute until evenly brown. Turn on to kitchen paper (paper towels) and leave to cool. Sprinkle with salt, if liked. Store in an airtight container.

Savoury salty nuts   Dry-roast the nuts (➤ *see page 79*), but sprinkle with 30 ml/2 tbsp soy sauce halfway through cooking, and toss well to coat.

Shelling hard-shelled nuts, such as brazils, almonds or walnuts   Soften them slightly by placing in a shallow dish with just enough water to cover. Microwave on High until the water boils. Remove from the oven immediately. Leave to stand for 1 minute, then drain. Spread out on kitchen paper (paper towels) to dry, then crack in the usual way.

Skinning hazelnuts (filberts)   Spread them in a single layer in a shallow dish. Microwave on High for 1½–2½ minutes. Tip into a clean tea towel (dish cloth) and rub off the skins.

Spiced roasted nuts   Dry-roast the nuts, as above, then sprinkle with sea salt and chilli powder to taste. Leave to cool, then store in an airtight container.

Toasting nuts   Use flaked (slivered) or chopped raw nuts. This method is also suitable for desiccated (shredded) coconut. Dry-roast (➤ *see page 79*), but take care, as being thinner and smaller the pieces can burn, so do not overcook. It is a good idea to stand a small cup of water in the oven with the nuts to absorb some of the energy.

➤ *see also Coatings, page 30, and Coconut, page 30*

Okra (ladies' fingers)

➤ *see Vegetables, pages 115–19*

Omelettes

➤ *see Eggs, page 41*

Onions

➤ *see Vegetables, pages 115–19*

It is not possible to fry (sauté) in the microwave but the following method makes a good substitute for fried onions. Chop or slice and place in a bowl with a generous knob of butter or margarine and a good sprinkling of light brown sugar. Cover with a small plate and cook on High for 2–4 minutes per onion, stirring twice during cooking until soft.

Onion sauce   Peel and chop a large onion. Place in a bowl with 30 ml/ 2 tbsp water. Cover and cook on High for 2–4 minutes until soft. Stir in 45 ml/3 tbsp plain (all-purpose) flour and blend in 250 ml/8 fl oz/1 cup milk. Add a small knob of butter. Microwave on High for 3–5 minutes, stirring after every minute until boiling and thickened. Season to taste and serve with lamb, pork, chicken or sausages. For a thinner sauce, use slightly less flour or thin with a little extra milk after cooking.

Orange curd

➤ *see Curds, page 36*

Oranges

➤ *see Fruit, Citrus, page 48, and Zest, page 125*

Caramelised oranges   Make a caramel (➤ *see Crème Caramel, page 35*) in a bowl. Pour in 150 ml/¼ pt/⅔ cup hot water (be careful as it may splutter). Stir well. Return to the microwave and cook on High for 1–2 minutes until the caramel dissolves, stirring once. Cut all the rind and pith off 4 oranges. Slice the fruit and place in the hot syrup. Cover and leave until cold, then chill before serving. Serves 4.

Oregano

➤ *see Herbs, Drying, page 55*

Ovenproof glassware

This is ideal for cooking in the microwave.

➤ *see also Dishes, page 37*

P

Paddles

Some microwave ovens have paddles, stirrers or antennae incorporated in the base or walls to encourage even distribution of the microwaves. Other makes have a turntable (➤ *see page 112*) to achieve a similar result.

Pancakes

These don't cook successfully in the microwave but they can be reheated. Place unfilled pancakes on a plate. Cover with kitchen paper (paper towels) or wrap in a napkin and heat for a few seconds on High until hot through; turn the stack over halfway through warming, if heating a pile of them. Alternatively, stuff in your usual way, cover the dish with greaseproof (waxed) paper and cook on High until piping hot through. Flour tortillas can be warmed in the same way.

➤ *see also Reheating, page 94*

Parsley

➤ *see Herbs, Drying, page 55*

Parsnips

➤ *see Vegetables, pages 115–19*

Partridge

➤ *see Poultry and Game, pages 86–8*

Pasta

Don't try and cook more than 450 g/1 lb pasta in one go. Place in a large casserole dish (Dutch oven). Cover with plenty of boiling water and add a pinch of salt. Stir well. Cover and microwave on High for the same time as you would when cooking conventionally, stirring once or twice during cooking. Leave to stand for 5 minutes, then drain and use as required.

Paste

➤ *see Pastry, below*

Pastry (paste)

A microwave oven will not brown or crisp pastry. It is, however, suitable for thawing pastry, making pastry cases (pie shells) and reheating cooked pastry dishes.

To thaw frozen blocks of puff or shortcrust (basic pie crust) Place in the microwave in its wrapper or unwrap and place on kitchen paper (paper towels) if more convenient. Microwave on Medium-Low for 1½–3 minutes, turning once. Leave to stand until completely thawed. Do not increase microwaving time or it will start to cook around the edges.

You can thaw and reheat cooked pastry dishes in one go. A 20 cm/8 in flan (pie), quiche or tart will take about 4 minutes on Medium-Low. Leave to stand for 5 minutes, then microwave on High for 3–4 minutes until ⊷ piping hot. The pastry should feel just warm, the filling will be hotter. To test, insert a knife down through the centre. Leave for 5 seconds, then remove: it should feel piping hot. If not, cook a minute or two longer.

➤ *see also Mince Pies, page 76, Quiches, page 92, and Sausage Rolls, page 100*

Puff and choux pastry These do not cook successfully as they need external heat to rise, crisp and brown. However, you can reheat or thaw pies, etc. made with them.

Shortcrust flan case (pie shell) Roll out 175 g/6 oz shortcrust pastry (basic pie crust). Use to line a 18 cm/7 in flan dish (pie pan). Prick the base with a fork and line with a double thickness of kitchen paper (paper towels). Cook on High for 3–5 minutes until just dry and beginning to shrink from the edges of the flan. Do not overcook or the pastry will toughen. Leave to stand for 2 minutes, then use as required.

Suet crust pastry Use for Dumplings (➤ *see page 38*), Roly-poly Pudding (➤ *see page 96*), and Suet Steamed Puddings (➤ *see page 106*).

Pavlova
➤ *see Meringues, page 74*

Peaches
➤ *see Fruit, page 47*

Pears
➤ *see Fruit, page 47*

Peas
➤ *see Vegetables, pages 115–19*

Pease pudding
Put 225 g/8 oz/1⅓ cups yellow split peas in a large bowl with just enough water to cover. Place in the microwave and cook on High for 4–5 minutes until the water boils. Leave to stand for 1 hour. Drain and return to the bowl. Add a finely chopped onion, 600 ml/1 pt/2½ cups ham or vegetable

stock, made with 1 stock cube, and a good grinding of black pepper. Cover with a plate. Cook on High for 20–30 minutes, stirring occasionally, until the peas are tender. If any liquid remains, remove the plate and cook on High for a few minutes more until evaporated and the mixture is pulpy. Season to taste before serving topped with crisp, crumbled bacon (➤ *see Bacon, page 11*). Serves 4.

Peppers (bell)

To skin peppers Cut into halves and remove the cores. Place cut sides down on a plate. Microwave on High for about 1 minute per half until the skin changes colour and begins to curl. Remove from the oven and when cool enough, pull off the skins.

Pie shell

➤ *see Biscuit Base, page 13, and Pastry (paste), page 82*

Pies

Pies can be reheated very successfully in a microwave. Pierce the top crust in several places with a sharp knife. Heat just until the pastry (paste) feels warm – the filling will be much hotter. Don't overheat or the pastry will become very soggy.

➤ *see also Reheating, page 94, and individual entries*

Pigeon

➤ *see Poultry and Game, pages 86–8*

Pitta breads

➤ *see Bread, page 16*

Pizza

For a crisp base, cook using a browning dish (➤ *see page 19*) or place on a microwave rack (➤ *see page 75*) over a plate (so that steam can circulate and stop the base getting too soggy). Microwave on High for 3–6 minutes. If making your own, cook with most of the topping ingredients on, but add the cheese for only the last 2 minutes' cooking time so that it doesn't toughen. For a brown top, place briefly under a hot grill (broiler) after cooking.

Leftover slices of pizza can be reheated successfully but they will be softer than when cooked conventionally. Place on a piece of kitchen paper (paper towel) and microwave on High for 15–20 seconds per slice. Test after 10 seconds. Do not overcook.

Pizza snacks Top split soft rolls, bagels or slices of French bread with a little tomato purée (paste), then chopped ham, sliced mushrooms, etc., and a pinch of dried mixed herbs or oregano. Place in a circle on a plate. Cover each with grated cheese and microwave on High just until the cheese melts. Serve straight away. Don't overcook or they will be tough.

Plaice

> ➤ *see Fish, page 43*

Plastic wrap

> ➤ *see Clingfilm, page 30*

Plated meals

One ready-plated meal of meat and vegetables with gravy will take 3–5 minutes on High. Always cover with a specially designed microwave lid, shallow dish or another plate before heating, and arrange foods with the thickest foods towards the outside. To heat more than one plate, use a set of microwave stacking rings, widely available from cook shops and hardware stores. For just two plates, place one on the base of the oven (or turntable if your oven has one), then one over the top on a microwave rack (➤ *see page 75*). Rearrange during cooking for even distribution of the microwaves.

To test if the meal is hot right through, hold your hand in the centre of the base of the plate. It should feel piping hot.

To cook from frozen, remove any foil and cover with a lid or upturned dish. Microwave on Medium-Low for 5 minutes, leave to stand for 2 minutes, then cook as above.

Plums

> ➤ *see Fruit, page 47*

Poaching

> ➤ *see Eggs, page 41, Fish, page 43, and Fruit, page 47*

Polenta

Only instant, precooked polenta is really successful in a microwave. Measure 225 g/8 oz/1⅓ cups instant polenta into a large dish. Stir in 1.2 litres/2 pts/5 cups boiling chicken or vegetable stock. Stir well. Cook on High for 7–9 minutes, stirring every 2 minutes until the mixture is thick and leaves the sides of the dish. When cooked, stir in 25 g/1 oz/ 2 tbsp butter or margarine, season with salt and freshly ground black pepper and sprinkle with grated Parmesan cheese and chopped parsley or basil before serving. Serves 4.

Poppadoms

Cook only one poppadum at a time. It is not necessary to brush them with oil. Lay one poppadom on a piece of kitchen paper (paper towel). Microwave on High for 10–20 seconds until beginning to puff up. Turn and cook until completely puffy.

20 / 30 seconds x 2

Pork

➤ *see Meat, page 71*

Porridge

Porridge cooks beautifully in the microwave and you will have no messy saucepan. Stir the required amount of rolled oats and water or milk (see packet instructions) in a bowl. Cook on High for 1 minute. Stir. Continue cooking, stirring every minute, until boiling, thickened and creamy. Leave to stand for 3 minutes. Season with salt and serve with milk or cream and sugar, if liked.

Potatoes

➤ *see Chips (fries), page 28, and Vegetables, pages 115–19*

Pottery

Most glazed pottery is ideal for cooking in the microwave but if you are unsure, do the Dish Test (➤ *see page 37*). For best results, soak in cold water before using.

Poultry and game

All types of poultry and game cook beautifully in the microwave, keeping them moist and tender. For best results, follow these general rules:

- All items must be thoroughly thawed before cooking in the microwave. Poultry with a cold spot in the centre won't cook properly and salmonella could multiply and cause severe food poisoning. Do not try to thaw a whole bird completely in the microwave (➤ *see Thawing Poultry, overleaf*).
- When casseroling poultry or game, remove the skin before cooking for better flavour and texture.
- Whole birds should be trussed. Shield wing tips and bone ends with thin strips of smooth foil.
- Stuff the neck, not the body cavity, of any poultry or game.
- Never salt the skin before cooking. It will draw out the moisture and toughen the flesh.
- Always give larger birds extra standing time halfway through cooking (➤ *see chart overleaf*).

- When cooking any bird over 1.5 kg/3 lb in weight, start by cooking with the breast down. Turn halfway through cooking.
- Rabbit casseroles benefit from being left overnight, then reheated to enhance the flavour (> see Reheating, page 94).
- Hare is rather tough to be cooked in the microwave and must be marinated first (> see chart below).
- When roasting birds, use a browning agent (> see page 18); paprika or soy sauce are particularly good for poultry.
- A roaster bag will also give excellent results (> see Covering Foods, page 33).
- After standing, test by piercing the thickest part of the thigh. If fully cooked, the juices should run clear.

Thawing poultry As I have already stated, it is not advisable to thaw whole birds by microwaving. Start the process in the microwave, then finish thawing naturally. For best results, follow these general rules:

- A bird is completely thawed when the giblets will pull out easily from the body cavity and no ice crystals remain.
- As a guide, allow 2 minutes per 450 g/1 lb on Medium-Low, then leave to stand. The whole process will take between 2 and 4 hours, compared with 8–12 hours when left to thaw naturally.
- In an emergency, you can thaw completely in the microwave if cooking straight away. Thaw on Low (not Medium-Low) for 10–20 minutes per 450 g/1 lb. Shield wing tips, legs and parson's nose with thin strips of foil and turn the bird frequently during thawing. Leave to stand for 1 hour after microwaving, then immediately cook the bird.
- Portions may be thawed completely. Place on a rack, cover with kitchen paper (paper towels) and thaw on Medium-Low, for 5–6 minutes per 450 g/1 lb, turning frequently. Wrap portions individually in foil after microwaving and leave to stand for 15 minutes before cooking.

Cooking poultry and game

Type of poultry or game	Preparation	Cooking time per 450 g/1 lb	Standing time
Chicken, whole	Stuff neck end if liked or put a sprig of herbs in the body cavity. Start cooking breast-down, turn halfway through.	5–8 minutes on Medium-High.	Wrap in foil, shiny side in, stand for 30 minutes.
Chicken portions	Brush with browning agent (see page 18) and place in a single layer in a roaster bag (see page 33).	5–8 minutes on Medium-High.	Wrap individually in foil, stand for 5 minutes.

Type of poultry or game	Preparation	Cooking time per 450 g/1 lb	Standing time
Capon	Stuff the neck end or place a whole lemon in the body cavity.	5–8 minutes on Medium-High	Stand for 30 minutes halfway through cooking. Wrap in foil and stand for 30 minutes at end.
Duckling	Put half an orange and onion inside. Prick the skin with a fork. Start breast-down, turn halfway through and drain off the fat completely.	7–9 minutes on Medium-High	Wrap in foil, shiny side in. Stand for 30 minutes. Crisp skin under a hot grill (broiler) if liked.
Duck portions	Prick the skin to drain the fat. Place in a single layer in a roaster bag (see page 33).	7–9 minutes on Medium-High	Wrap individually in foil. Stand for 10 minutes.
Grouse	Stuff each with a small onion studded with a clove.	8–10 minutes on Medium	Wrap individually in foil. Stand for 15 minutes.
Guinea fowl	Stuff cavity with a slice of lemon and a small bay leaf.	8–10 minutes on Medium	Wrap in foil, shiny side in. Stand for 15 minutes.
Patridge	Stuff with an apple and herb stuffing.	8½–12 minutes on Medium	Wrap in foil, shiny side in. Stand for 15 minutes.
Pheasant	Put an onion, studded with a clove, and a small bay leaf inside. Cover the breast with bacon.	8½–12 minutes on Medium-High	Wrap in foil shiny side in. Stand for 15 minutes.
Pigeon	Marinate in Red Wine Marinade (see page 69) in a casserole dish (Dutch oven). Cook in marinade.	12–15 minutes for two birds on Medium	Stand for 5 minutes.
Poussin	Leave whole or spatchcock (split in half down backbone and open out flat). Cook up to four in one go.	5–8 minutes on Medium-High	Wrap individually in foil, shiny side in. Stand for 30 minutes.
Rabbit	Casserole only. Prepare in the usual way (see Casseroles, page 25).	50 minutes to 1 hour per rabbit on Medium	Stand for 5 minutes. Season before serving.
Turkey	Up to 4.5 kg/10 lb only. Stuff neck with sausagemeat or stuffing. Cook breast-down first.	5–8 minutes on Medium-High	Wrap in foil. Stand for 30 minutes.

Power output settings

There is no standard power indicator on microwave ovens, but it's the percentage output you use that is important. So, for instance, when using 100 per cent output, some manufacturers call this High (as I have in this book) or Full Power and others have the actual maximum wattage output on the dial or programmer e.g. 1000 watts. This chart will help you find the right settings.

Power settings for a 1000 watt oven

Percentage	Description	Number on dial	Wattage
10%	Low, Warm	1	100 watts
30%	Medium-Low, Defrost	2	300 watts
50%	Medium, Simmer	3	500 watts
70%	Medium-High, Roast	4	700 watts
100%	High, Full Power	5	1000 watts

There are five different power levels on most ovens. Many foods are best when cooked on High (100 per cent). But if you have a high wattage oven, you may get better results cooking on Medium-High (70 per cent) because the microwaves are so fierce. Check your manufacturer's instructions, and try both ways to see which results are best. In all cookers, some foods benefit from more gentle cooking as follows:

Using the settings

Percentage	Suitable for
High (100%)	Quick cooking of bacon rashers (slices), tender poultry or steaks, fish, fruit, vegetables, bread, cakes and puddings; reheating leftovers; heating a browning dish (see page 19).
Medium-High (70%)	Cakes and puddings; roasting meat and poultry; cooking and reheating bread; especially useful for high-wattage cookers.
Medium (50%)	Simmering stews and casseroles, soups, eggs, cream and cheese dishes; reheating frozen meals.
Medium-Low (30%)	Thawing; slow-cooking curries and casseroles; cooking custards; softening butter and cheese.
Low (10%)	Keeping foods warm; infusing milk and sauces for flavour; very gentle thawing.

➤ see also Labelling, page 63

Prawns (shrimp)

➤ see Fish, page 44

Probe

➤ see Microwave Thermometer, page 75

Proving bread

➤ see Bread, page 16

Prunes

➤ see Fruit, Dried, page 48

Puddings

➤ see individual entries

Eve's pudding. Use sponge recipe on p.24. & proceed as usual. Microwave on 100 for 4 min, then transfer for 15 min. to oven at 370°C.

Puff pastry (paste)

➤ see Pastry (paste), page 82

Pulses

All pulses, except red lentils, should be soaked for several hours or overnight in cold water before microwaving. The only advantages of cooking in the microwave rather than conventionally are that they won't boil dry and burn and you won't steam up the kitchen. Drain after soaking, place in a very large bowl and cover with enough boiling water to come 2.5 cm/1 in above the beans. Microwave on High for 30 minutes. Stir. Don't use a lower setting as the water must boil rapidly during cooking to destroy any toxins in the beans. Test for tenderness, then continue to cook in 5-minute bursts until tender but still holding their shape. Stir every 5 minutes. Season with salt, if liked, leave to stand for 5 minutes, then drain and use as required.

For red lentils, cover with boiling water and cook for 20 minutes. Test and cook a little longer if necessary until tender. Season with salt, if liked, leave to stand for 5 minutes, then drain and use as required.

➤ see also Pease Pudding, page 83

Q

Quantities

If you want to cook a smaller or larger quantity of food than a microwave recipe states, the time it takes in the microwave will vary. So for half the quantity of food, you do not simply halve the cooking time. For best results, follow these general rules.

When cooking a smaller quantity than stated:
- Use a smaller dish.
- If cooking half the quantity, reduce the cooking time by about one third. If cooking a quarter of the quantity, reduce the cooking time by about two-thirds. So, if a recipe makes 4 servings and takes 12 minutes to cook, enough for 2 servings will take about 8 minutes, enough for 1 serving will take about 4 minutes.
- Reduce standing time in the same way.
- As always, cook for a little less time than you calculate, test, then add on more time in short bursts, testing as you go. Once you know the timings of a particular recipe, note them down so you don't forget.
- If cooking very small amounts of food – like a small amount of chocolate or one wedge of pizza – put a cup of water in the microwave alongside the food. It will absorb some of the energy, preventing the food from overheating too quickly.

When increasing quantities:
- Use a larger dish.
- If you increase the quantity of food by a half, increase the cooking time by about a third. If doubling the quantity, increase the cooking time by a half. So, if 4 servings takes 12 minutes, allow 16 minutes for 6 servings. If making enough to serve 8, cook for about 18 minutes.
- Increase standing time in the same way.
- Again, cook for less time than expected, check, then add on extra time in short bursts, testing as you go.
- Microwave ovens don't make a good job of cooking huge quantities. The microwaves need to penetrate as much of the food as possible, so there must be room to stir food or rearrange it. A very thick joint, for instance, is likely to overcook on the outside before the centre is cooked, even if you turn it over during cooking, as the same part of the food is being continually blasted. Removing the food to stand for some time, halfway through cooking, can help overcome this.

- Remember, the bigger the quantity, the longer it takes. So if, for instance, you wanted to bake 12 large potatoes and a large casserole for a party, it would make more sense to use the conventional cooker and do it all in one go, than try to cook it all in the microwave!

Queen scallops

> *see Fish, page 44*

Quiches

Make a shortcrust pastry case (pie shell). Fill with your chosen ingredients and cover with grated Cheddar cheese, if liked. Beat 2 eggs with 300 ml/½ pt/1¼ cups milk and a little seasoning. Pour over. Bake on Medium for 15–20 minutes or until the filling is set. Place under a hot grill (broiler) to brown, if liked.

Thawing Remove any foil packaging. Place on a plate and cook on Medium-Low for 6–8 minutes for a family-sized flan, 2–3 minutes for a small one.

Reheating Remove any foil packaging and cook on Medium for 2½–4 minutes for a family-sized flan, 30 seconds to 1½ minutes for a small one.

> *see also Pastry (paste), page 82*

Quorn

> *see Burgers, page 21*

Rabbit

> ➤ see Poultry and Game, pages 86–8

Rack

> ➤ see Microwave Rack, page 75

Raisins

> ➤ see Fruit, Dried, page 48

Raspberries

> ➤ see Fruit, page 47

Ratatouille

Prepare the vegetables in your usual way. Cook the onion in the oil in a casserole dish (Dutch oven) for 2–3 minutes until softened. Stir in the remaining ingredients. Cover and cook on High for 8–12 minutes or until cooked to your liking, stirring twice. Season to taste and leave to stand for 3–4 minutes before serving.

Recipe conversion

Most conventional recipes can be cooked in the microwave, but you will need to experiment to get the best from your machine. See tips throughout this book for specific dishes and follow these general rules:

- For soups and casseroles, use only two-thirds the amount of liquid. Don't use tough cuts of meat. Cut meat into 2.5 cm/1 in cubes and divide poultry into even-sized portions. Cut up any vegetables into small, even-sized pieces.
- Cut the conventional cooking time by three-quarters if cooking on High.
- Cut the conventional cooking time in half if cooking on Medium.
- Cut the conventional cooking time by a quarter if cooking on Medium-Low.
- Cover a dish in the microwave if you would cover it in your conventional oven.
- Remember that food will continue to cook during standing time, so don't overcook.

Red kidney beans

> ➤ see Pulses, page 90

Red lentils

> see Pulses, page 90

Red mullet

> see Fish, page 43

Redcurrants

> see Fruit, page 47

Reheating

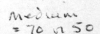

Many foods can be reheated successfully in the microwave. Ready-made dishes like Lasagne, Shepherd's Pie, etc. are best reheated on Medium, if cooking from frozen; if they have been stored in the fridge, reheat on High. In all cases, heat until piping hot throughout. Test by pushing a knife down through the centre and holding it for 5 seconds, then remove. If the blade feels piping hot, the dish is ready. If not, cook for a few minutes more.

> see also individual entries, Convenience Foods, page 32, and
> Plated Meals, page 85

Reheating drinks

To reheat hot drinks that have gone cold, place the mug or cup in the microwave and microwave on High for 1–2 minutes until hot through. Stir before serving to distribute the heat. Make sure the mug is microwave safe before heating.

Rhubarb

> see Fruit, page 47

Rice

All types of rice cook and reheat extremely well in a microwave.

Brown rice Wash 165 g/6 oz/¾ cup brown long-grain rice, drain and place in a casserole dish (Dutch oven). Add 400 ml/14 fl oz/3¾ cups water and a good pinch of salt. Stir well. Cover. Microwave on High for 2–4 minutes. Reduce to Medium and cook for a further 25–40 minutes, stirring twice, until tender but still nutty. Leave to stand for 3 minutes, then fluff up and serve. Serves 4.

Long-grain rice Wash 225 g/8 oz/1 cup long-grain rice thoroughly. Drain and place in a large casserole dish (Dutch oven). Add 600 ml/ 1 pt/2½ cups boiling water and a good pinch of salt. Stir well. Cover and cook on High for 10–14 minutes, stirring twice. Leave to stand for 3 minutes until the rice has absorbed the liquid. Serves 4.

Mediterranean tomato rice   Prepare as Long-grain Rice (➤ *see page 95*) but add half water and a 400 g/14 oz/large can of chopped tomatoes instead of all water. Stir in 15 ml/1 tbsp tomato purée (paste). Stand, then stir in 15 ml/1 tbsp chopped basil before serving.

Reheating rice   Put the cooked rice in a casserole dish (Dutch oven). Cover and heat on High for 3–5 minutes, stirring twice, until piping hot. Add 15–30 ml/1–2 tbsp water to the rice, if liked, to keep it moist.

Savoury rice   Cook as Long-grain Rice (➤ *see page 95*) but crumble a chicken, beef or vegetable stock cube in with the boiling water.

Scented yellow rice   Prepare as Long-grain Rice (➤ *see page 95*), but add 5 ml/1 tsp turmeric, 1 small bay leaf, a 2.5 cm/1 in piece of cinnamon stick and 4 split cardamom pods with the water. Remove the whole herbs and spices before serving, if liked.

Vegetable rice   Prepare as for Savoury Rice, but add 100 g/4 oz diced frozen mixed vegetables with the boiling water and cook for an extra 1–2 minutes.

Rice pudding

For best results, soak the rice in the milk overnight. Put 50 g/2 oz/¼ cup round-grain (pudding) rice in a large bowl. Stir in a 410 g/14 oz/large can of evaporated milk and a canful of water. Stir in 30 ml/2 tbsp sugar. Microwave on High for 4–6 minutes, stirring once until boiling. Reduce to Medium and cook for 30–40 minutes, stirring twice until thick and creamy. Stir well again and leave to stand for 5 minutes before serving. Dust with a little grated nutmeg if liked. Serves 4.

➤ *see also Milk Puddings, page 76*

Ripening cheese
➤ *see Cheese, page 26*

Roaster bags
➤ *see Covering Foods, page 33*

Roasting meat
➤ *see Meat, pages 71–4*

Roasting poultry
➤ *see Poultry and Game, pages 86–8*

Rock salmon
➤ *see Fish, page 43*

Rolls

> see Bread, page 16

Roly-poly pudding

Filled, rolled suet puddings cook well in the microwave. Make in your usual way, wrap loosely in double-thickness greaseproof (waxed) paper or non-stick baking parchment (to allow for rising), and twist the ends to seal. Microwave on High for about 4–6 minutes or until a skewer inserted in the centre comes out clean. If still slightly soft, cook for another 1–2 minutes.

> see also Suet Steamed Puddings, page 106

Rosemary

> see Herbs, Drying, page 55

Rum and raisin ice cream

> see Ice Cream, page 57

Rutabaga

> see Vegetables, pages 115–19

Safety

Although microwaving is a very safe form of cooking, there are a few safety rules that you should always follow:

● Never switch on the microwave with nothing in it. It could damage it. To make sure this never happens, leave a cup of water inside the cooker when not in use.

● Wear oven gloves when lifting out large bowls, casseroles, etc. of hot food especially those high in sugar such as jam (conserve) and chutney.

● Keep your microwave oven clean. Dirty door seals could allow microwaves to escape.

➢ *see also Burning, page 21, and Cleaning Your Microwave, page 29*

Sage

➢ *see Herbs, Drying, page 55*

Salmon

➢ *see Fish, page 43*

Salsify

➢ *see Vegetables, pages 115–19*

Salt

Never use salt to season meat, fish, poultry or vegetables before cooking. It draws out the moisture and can toughen the food.

Sauce, apple

➢ *see Apples, page 7*

Sauce, Béarnaise

➢ *see Sauces, Egg-based, page 98*

Sauce, bread

➢ *see Bread, page 16*

Sauce, cheese

➢ *see Sauces, Milk-based, page 99*

Sauce, chocolate

➢ *see Sauces, Milk-based, page 99*

Sauce, cranberry

➤ *see Cranberries, page 34*

Sauce, custard

➤ *see Sauces, Milk-based, page 99*

Sauce, Hollandaise

➤ *see Sauces, Egg-based, below*

Sauce, onion

➤ *see Onions, page 81*

Sauce, parsley

➤ *see Sauces, Milk-based, page 99*

Sauce, tomato

➤ *see Tomatoes, page 112*

Sauce, vanilla

➤ *see Sauces, Milk-based, page 99*

Sauce, white

➤ *see Sauces, Milk-based, page 99*

Sauces, egg-based

Egg-based sauces are easier to make in the microwave than conventionally. The trick is not to cook for too long between whisking or the mixture will curdle.

Béarnaise sauce   Make as for Hollandaise Sauce (➤ *see below*), but use white wine vinegar instead of the lemon juice and add 15 ml/1 tbsp fresh chopped tarragon with the seasonings.

Hollandaise sauce   Cut 100 g/4 oz/½ cup butter into small pieces and place in a large bowl. Cover with a sheet of kitchen paper (paper towel) and microwave on High for 30–50 seconds or until almost melted. Stir to complete the melting. Add 30 ml/2 tbsp lemon juice and 2 eggs. Whisk until thoroughly blended. Microwave on High for 1 minute. Whisk again Continue to microwave, whisking every 15 seconds until thickened, smooth and glossy. Season to taste and serve.

Sauces, milk-based

Microwaving is very suitable for making milk-based sauces and saves washing up as all the ingredients are mixed in the serving dish or jug.

NB · Check after 3 min ? reduce time
in stirring

Basic white sauce   Blend 30 ml/2 tbsp cornflour (cornstarch) with a little milk taken from 300 ml/½ pt/1¼ cups in a bowl. Blend in the remaining milk. Add a small knob of butter or margarine. Cook in the microwave on High for 1 minute. Whisk well. Cook in 1-minute bursts until boiling, thickened and smooth. Cook for 1 further minute. Season with salt and pepper or sweeten with sugar.

Cheese sauce   Prepare as for Basic White Sauce (➢ *see above*), but whisk in 50g/2 oz/½ cup grated Cheddar cheese before seasoning with salt and pepper.

Chocolate sauce   Prepare as for Basic White Sauce (➢ *see above*), but substitute 15 ml/1 tbsp of the cornflour (cornstarch) with cocoa (unsweetened chocolate) powder and sweeten to taste with sugar.

(crème patissière)

Confectioners' custard   Blend 150 ml/¼ pt/⅔ cup milk with 15 ml/1 tbsp caster (superfine) sugar and 15 ml/1 tbsp cornflour (cornstarch). Microwave on High for 1 minute. Whisk well and microwave for a further 1–1½ minutes until really thick. Whisk in 1 egg yolk and 1.5 ml/¼ tsp vanilla essence (extract). Microwave on High for 1–2 minutes, whisking after every 30 seconds until very thick. Cook for a further 30 seconds, if necessary. Beat in a good knob of butter or margarine. Cover with a circle of wetted greaseproof (waxed) paper to stop a skin forming and leave until cold. Use as required.

Custard sauce   Blend 30 ml/2 tbsp custard powder with 30 ml/2 tbsp caster (superfine) sugar and a little milk from 300 ml/½ pt/1¼ cups milk. Blend in the remaining milk. Cook on High until thick and bubbling, whisking after every minute. Whisk in a little more milk if a thinner custard is required.

Parsley sauce   Prepare as for Basic White Sauce (➢ *see above*), but whisk in 30 ml/2 tbsp chopped parsley before seasoning with salt and pepper.

Traditional white sauce   Melt 20 g/¾ oz/1½ tbsp butter or margarine in a bowl in the microwave on High for 30–40 seconds. Blend in 20 g/¾ oz/ 3 tbsp plain (all-purpose) flour. Gradually whisk in 300 ml/½ pt/1¼ cups milk. Return to the microwave and cook for 1 minute. Whisk and return to the oven. Continue cooking, whisking every minute until boiling and thickened. Season to taste. Flavour as required.

Vanilla sauce   Prepare as for Basic White Sauce (➢ *see above*), but add vanilla essence (extract) and sugar to taste. If liked, whisk in a whole egg before cooking and thin with extra milk, if necessary.

Sausage rolls

To reheat cooked sausage rolls, place on a piece of kitchen paper (paper towel) and heat on High for 15 seconds per sausage roll. To re-crisp the pastry (paste), place briefly under a hot grill (broiler) if liked.

Sausages

➤ *see Meat, pages 71–4, and Smoked Pork Rings, page 102*

Sautéing   P·74

➤ *see Frying, page 49, and Stir-frying, page 105*

Scallops

➤ *see Fish, page 44*

Scones (biscuits)

Plain, white scones can be cooked on a browning dish (➤ *see page 19*) to give a golden colour and crisp crust.

Cheese scones   Mix 100 g/4 oz/1 cup wholemeal self-raising (self-rising) flour and 100 g/4 oz/1 cup white self-raising flour, 5 ml/1 tsp baking powder and a pinch of salt in a bowl. Stir in 5 ml/1 tsp dry mustard. Rub in 40 g/1½ oz/3 tbsp butter or margarine. Stir in 50 g/2 oz/½ cup grated red Cheddar cheese. Add a squeeze of lemon juice and enough milk to form a soft but not sticky dough. Knead gently on a lightly floured surface and pat out to about 2 cm/¾ in thick. Cut into eight rounds using a 5 cm/2 in biscuit (cookie) cutter, then place in a circle on a piece of greaseproof (waxed) paper on a plate. Microwave on High for 1–2 minutes, then turn, brush with water and sprinkle with grated cheese. Microwave for a further 1–2 minutes until risen and spongy. Leave to stand for 2 minutes, then transfer to a wire rack to cool.

Sweet scones   Mix 100 g/4 oz/1 cup wholemeal self-raising (self-rising) flour and 100 g/4 oz/1 cup white self-raising flour in a bowl. Stir in 5 ml/ 1 tsp baking powder, a pinch of salt and 50 g/2 oz/¼ cup light brown sugar. Rub in 50 g/2 oz/¼ cup butter or margarine. Add a squeeze of lemon juice, then mix with enough milk to form a soft but not sticky dough. Knead gently on a lightly floured surface. Pat out to about 2 cm/¾ in thick. Cut into eight rounds using a 5 cm/2 in biscuit (cookie) cutter and place in a circle on a piece of greaseproof (waxed) paper on a plate. Microwave on High for 1–2 minutes. Turn over and brush with melted butter and sprinkle with demerara sugar. Microwave for a further 1–2 minutes until risen and spongy. Leave to stand for 2 minutes, then transfer to a wire rack to cool.

Seasonings

➤ *see Salt, page 97, and Flavourings, page 46*

Sesame seeds, toasted

Put in an even layer on a plate. Microwave on High, checking and stirring every few seconds until browned. Store in an airtight container. Use to coat foods (➤ *see Coatings, page 30*) and to add flavour to many sweet and savoury dishes. If toasting only a small amount, put a small cup of water in the microwave at the same time to absorb some of the energy.

Settings

➤ *see Power Output Settings, page 89*

Shellfish

➤ *see Fish, page 44*

Shepherd's/cottage pie

Peel and cut up 750 g/1½ lb potatoes. Cook in the microwave (➤ *see Vegetables, page 115*) or cook conventionally. Drain and mash with a knob of butter, a dash of milk and seasoning to taste. Chop an onion and place in a flameproof serving dish. Add 350 g/12 oz minced (ground) lamb or beef. Cover and microwave on High for 3–5 minutes, stirring twice, until the meat is no longer pink and all the grains are separate. Add 300 ml/ ½ pt/1¼ cups lamb or beef stock, a bouquet garni sachet and 50 g/2 oz frozen peas. Microwave on High for 5–8 minutes, stirring twice, until tender. Blend 30 ml/2 tbsp plain (all-purpose) flour with a little water and stir in. Microwave, uncovered, for 2–3 minutes until thickened, stirring once. Remove the bouquet garni sachet and season to taste. Spoon the potato all over the top of the meat. Roughen the top with a fork. Place under a hot grill (broiler) until browned. Serves 4.

➤ *see also Reheating, page 94*

Shielding

Use small strips of foil to shield, or protect, wing tips, bone ends or fish tails from overcooking. The foil reflects the microwaves, stopping them from penetrating the food.

➤ *see also Foil, page 46*

Shortbread

Softer biscuits (cookies) which don't need to be brown, such as shortbread, cook well in the microwave.

Soften 100 g/4 oz/½ cup butter or margarine in a bowl on Low for 30 seconds. Beat in 50 g/2 oz/¼ cup caster (superfine) sugar until fluffy.

Sift 150 g/5 oz/1¼ cups plain (all-purpose) flour and 25 g/1 oz/3 tbsp semolina (cream of wheat) over the surface. Work in with a wooden spoon to form a dough. Knead gently on a lightly floured surface, then press into an 18 cm/7 in flan dish (pie pan), base-lined with non-stick baking parchment. Prick all over with a fork. Bake on High for 4–6 minutes until just firm. Leave to stand for 5 minutes. Mark into six or eight pieces, then leave to cool completely before cutting.

Shrimps

➤ see Fish, page 43

Skinning fruit

➤ see Fruit, page 48

Smoked fish

➤ see Fish, page 43

Smoked pork rings

Place in their package in a shallow dish. Pierce the bag and the skin of the sausages in several places. Microwave on High for 1–2 minutes, turn and cook for a further 1–2 minutes until piping hot. Stand for 2 minutes. Remove with oven gloves. Slice and serve piping hot.

Snow peas

➤ see Vegetables, pages 115–19

Soda bread

➤ see Bread, page 17

Sole

➤ see Fish, page 43

Soup

Most soups can be made successfully in the microwave. For best results, follow these general rules:

- Use a large container so the liquid doesn't boil over.
- Reduce the amount of liquid stated in the recipe by up to half, as there is less evaporation.
- Keep seasonings to a minimum, then taste and add extra at the end of cooking.
- Cook on High, stirring occasionally, until the ingredients are soft. Leave to stand for 5 minutes.

Soused herrings

➤ *see Fish, page 44*

Soused mackerel

➤ *see Fish, page 44*

Spaghetti

➤ *see Pasta, page 82*

Spaghetti Bolognese

➤ *see Bolognese Sauce, page 15*

Spinach

➤ *see Vegetables, pages 115–19*

Spring (collard) greens

➤ *see Vegetables, pages 115–19*

Split peas

➤ *see Pulses, page 90*

Sponge cake

➤ *see Cakes, Sponge, page 23*

Sponge puddings

To make Plain Sponge Pudding, prepare as for Basic Sponge Cake (➤ *see page 24*) but place in a very lightly greased 1.2 litre/2 pt/5 cup pudding basin, base-lined with a circle of non-stick baking parchment. Place on a microwave rack (➤ *see page 75*) or upturned small plate and cook on High for 4–6 minutes until just shrinking from the sides of the bowl and the top still has a few moist spots. Leave to stand for 5 minutes, turn out and serve with Jam Sauce (➤ *see page 59*) and Custard Sauce (➤ *see page 99*).

Chocolate sponge pudding Prepare as for Plain Sponge Pudding (➤ *see above*) but use the Chocolate Cake mixture (➤ *see page 28*). Serve with Chocolate Sauce (➤ *see page 99*).

Sultana sponge pudding Prepare as for Plain Sponge Pudding (➤ *see above*) but add 50 g/2 oz/⅓ cup sultanas (golden raisins) to the cake mixture and 2.5 ml/½ tsp mixed (apple-pie) spice. Serve with Custard Sauce (➤ *see page 99*).

Syrup sponge pudding Put 45 ml/3 tbsp golden (light corn) syrup in the basin before adding the Basic Sponge Cake mixture (➤ *see page 24*). Add the finely grated rind of ½ lemon to the mixture, if liked. Serve with warmed golden (light corn) syrup (➤ *see page 51*) and Custard Sauce (➤ *see page 99*).

Upside-down pudding Line the base of a round, 20 cm/8 in, shallow dish with non-stick baking parchment. Melt 25 g/1 oz/2 tbsp butter in the dish on High for 30 seconds. Tilt to spread the butter around. Sprinkle liberally with 45 ml/3 tbsp light brown sugar. Open a 320 g/12 oz/ medium can of pineapple slices, or a 410 g/14½ oz/large can of peach, apricot or pear halves. Pour 30 ml/2 tbsp of the juice over the sugar. Arrange the slices of fruit in the base, and decorate with glacé (candied) cherries and angelica leaves in the gaps. Spoon the Basic Sponge Cake mixture (➤ *see page 24*) over and level the surface. Place on an upturned plate or a microwave rack (➤ *see page 75*) and microwave on High for 5–8 minutes or until the sponge is risen and shrinking from the sides of the dish. There may still be a few wet spots on the top. Leave to stand for 10 minutes. Turn out, remove the paper and serve with Custard Sauce (➤ *see page 99*) or cream.

Sprouts, Brussels
➤ *see Vegetables, pages 115–19*

Squash
➤ *see Vegetables, pages 115–19*

Standing time
Microwaves cook by causing the water molecules in the food to vibrate, creating friction which, in turn, creates heat. Consequently, food continues to cook when taken out of the oven while the vibration gradually slows down and stops. For this reason, food is usually taken out of the microwave to complete cooking during a specified standing time. That is why foods may seem undercooked when first removed.

It is always better to undercook food, then, if necessary, give a few minutes' more cooking after standing time. Once food is overcooked the problem cannot be rectified.

Insulating food In order that the food remains piping hot and continues to cook while standing, it should be insulated to retain the heat. Wrap in foil, shiny side in, or if in a covered dish, put a clean tea towel (dish cloth) over for the duration of the standing time.

Stem lettuce

> ➤ see Chinese Leaves, page 28, and Vegetables, pages 115–19

Sterilising

To sterilise jars for preserving foods, put 150 ml/¼ pt/⅔ cup water in each clean jar. Microwave on High until the water is boiling, then continue to microwave for 1 minute. Remove from the oven using oven gloves. Pour out the water and stand the jars upside down on kitchen paper (paper towels) to drain. Use while hot if adding hot preserves or allow the preserve to cool before putting into cool jars.

The microwave should NOT be used to sterilise baby equipment (➤ see Baby Food, page 11).

Stir-frying

Stir-frying in the microwave takes about the same amount of time as cooking conventionally but less stirring is needed and cooking smells and any splattering are kept to a minimum. There is also no risk of burning the food. For best results, follow these general rules:

- Cut foods into even-sized pieces.
- There is no need to heat the oil first. Simply toss the foods to be cooked in a little oil in a large, shallow dish.
- If using meat, cook for 2–3 minutes on High, stirring once, until almost cooked before adding vegetables.
- Add first the vegetables that take longest to cook e.g. onions, carrots, celery, then add the remainder, e.g. green beans, (bell) peppers, cucumber, mushrooms, beansprouts, stirring every minute until cooked to your liking.
- Add any seasonings, such as soy sauce, spices, sherry, etc. at the end of cooking.
- A vegetable stir-fry for 4 people will take about 4–6 minutes, a meat and vegetable stir-fry about 6–9 minutes.
- If adding Chinese noodles, cook according to the packet instructions, drain and add at the end of cooking. Microwave on High for 1 minute to heat through. Toss and serve.

Stirrers

> ➤ see Paddles, page 82

Stirring

It is important to stir and turn food during cooking to distribute the microwaves evenly. All recipes tell you when to do this. Also, remember always to stir reheated drinks before sipping. The surface will be scalding, even if the liquid is cooler underneath.

➤ *see also Arranging Foods for Cooking, page 8, and Turning, page 112*

Stock

Stock can be made very easily in the microwave, cutting down on the smells and condensation caused by lengthy conventional cooking.

Put the stock ingredients in a large casserole dish (Dutch oven) with just enough boiling water to cover. Make sure there is plenty of head room to avoid boiling over. Cover and microwave on High for 7–10 minutes for fish stock, 16–20 minutes for chicken stock and 35–45 minutes for meat bone stock. Season with salt and freshly ground black pepper after cooking. Leave to stand until cold before skimming and straining.

Suet steamed puddings

Prepare as for conventional cooking, leaving at least 2.5 cm/1 in at the top of the basin to allow for rising. Cover with a dome of double-thickness greaseproof (waxed) paper, twisting and folding under the rim to secure. Place on a microwave rack (➤ *see page 75*) or upturned plate. Microwave on High for about 6–8 minutes until risen and cooked through. Leave to stand for 5 minutes. Either tie a napkin round the basin, or loosen the edges and turn out on to a plate before serving.

➤ *see also Roly-poly Pudding, page 96*

Sugar

Brown sugars are very useful for adding colour and flavour, particularly to cakes cooked in a microwave. But they can go hard if not used.

To soften, place the block in a casserole dish (Dutch oven). Add a slice of bread or apple or sprinkle lightly with water. Cover and microwave on High for 30–50 seconds. Leave to stand for 5 minutes, remove the bread or apple, then break up the sugar and use or store in an airtight container.

To dry out damp sugar, empty 100 g/4 oz/½ cup damp sugar into a bowl. Microwave on High for 20–40 seconds. Stir well.

Sugar snap peas

Cook as for mangetout (snow peas).

➤ *see Vegetables, pages 115–19*

Sultanas (golden raisins)

> see Fruit, Dried, page 48

Swede (rutabaga)

> see Vegetables, pages 115–19

Sweetcorn (corn)

> see Vegetables, pages 115–19

Syrups, sugar

To make a light syrup, stir 100 g/4 oz/½ cup granulated sugar in 300 ml/ ½ pt/1¼ cups water. Add a thick slice of lemon. Microwave on High for 4–5 minutes, stirring every minute until boiling. Remove the lemon. Use as required.

Brown syrup   Prepare as above, but use light brown sugar instead of granulated.

Cider syrup   Prepare as above, but use medium cider instead of water.

Heavy syrup   Prepare as above, but use 175 g/6 oz sugar.

Mulled syrup   Prepare as for any of the above syrups but add a 5 cm/2 in piece of cinnamon stick, 2 cloves and a piece of star anise (optional) while cooking. Remove before use.

Red wine syrup   Prepare as above, but substitute red wine (or half wine and half water) for the water.

White wine syrup   Prepare as for Red Wine Syrup (above) but use a fruity white wine instead of red.

> see also Golden (Light Corn) Syrup, page 51

T

Tabbouleh

Cook 225 g/8 oz/2 cups bulgar (cracked) wheat (➤ *see page 21*). Stir in 60 ml/4 tbsp each of olive oil and lemon juice and leave to cool. Just before serving, stir in ¼ chopped cucumber, 4 chopped tomatoes, 1 chopped green (bell) pepper, 1 crushed garlic clove, 30 ml/2 tbsp chopped parsley and a good grinding of black pepper. Toss and serve. Serves 6.

Tarragon

➤ *see Herbs, Drying, page 55*

Tarts

➤ *see Pastry (paste), page 82*

Tea

To make 1 cup, put a tea bag in a mug and top up with cold water. Microwave on High until the water boils. Leave to stand for 1 minute. Stir, remove the bag and add milk or a slice of lemon, to taste.

➤ *see also Reheating Drinks, page 94*

Temperature

The temperature of food before it is put in the microwave will affect the cooking time. Food taken straight from the fridge will take longer to reheat or cook than foods at room temperature. Some foods, such as vegetables or fish can be cooked from frozen. They will, of course, take longer than thawed or fresh foods. See individual entries.

➤ *see also Meat Temperature Chart, page 73*

Temperature probe

➤ *see Microwave Thermometer, page 75*

Thawing   "POWER OUTPUT" P-89

Many microwave ovens now have an automatic defrost function. You enter details of the food (e.g. type of meat, weight, etc.) and the oven will pulse energy on and off, with standing time built in. Simply follow the manufacturer's instructions.

Thawing is usually carried out at 30 per cent power. Unlike cooking on High, the timing varies very little whatever the output of your model. The rules for arranging, size and shape of food apply to thawing as well as cooking, but also remember the following general rules:

- If thawing meat or foods where you don't want to use the liquid that drips out, place on a microwave rack (➤ *see page 75*) with a container underneath so the liquid will drip away from the food.
- Thaw in short bursts only, with standing time in between. If you microwave for too long, you'll start to cook the outside.
- Check food before the end of the calculated thawing time and remember it will continue to defrost during standing.
- When thawing minced (ground) meat, scrape off the meat as it thaws and remove from the oven. Free-flow mince can be cooked from frozen – no thawing is necessary.
- Break up casseroles, soups or other foods frozen in a block as they thaw and move the still-frozen pieces to the outside of the dish.
- Ease apart chops, diced meat, sliced bread, bacon rashers (slices), etc. as they thaw to allow more even distribution of the microwaves.
- If thawing food such as frozen peas in a bag, flex the bag occasionally to distribute the microwaves evenly.
- Don't try to defrost whole joints or poultry completely. Start the process in the microwave, then leave at room temperature, wrapped in foil, shiny side in, to finish thawing. Salmonella, a nasty form of food poisoning, can occur if the flesh starts to cook before it is completely thawed. Poultry portions, steaks and chops can be thawed completely in the microwave.
- Protect bone ends and thin ends of meat, poultry or fish as they thaw with tiny strips of smooth foil, to protect them from beginning to cook while the rest of the food completes thawing.
- Put cakes, bread and desserts on a piece of kitchen paper (paper towel) to absorb moisture as they thaw.
- Don't try to defrost large cream desserts, such as cheesecakes completely. Again, start the process in the microwave, then let it thaw completely at room temperature.
- Remove any metal twist ties or lids before thawing in the microwave.
- Vegetables can be cooked straight from frozen. Bags of frozen peas, for instance, can be cooked in their bag.

> ➤ *see also Cooking Frozen Vegetables, page 119, Cream Cakes, Thawing, page 34, Meat Thawing Times, page 73, and Thawing Poultry, page 87*

Thawing cooked dishes

Cooked dishes such as Lasagne, Moussaka, Shepherd's Pie, etc. can be thawed and reheated in one operation provided they were frozen in a microwave-safe dish. Cook on Medium. Turn the dish once or twice during cooking to avoid hot and cold spots. Test the food is piping hot throughout by inserting a knife down through the centre. Hold for 5 seconds, then remove: the blade should be burning hot. If not, heat for a little longer.

➤ *see also Quiches, page 92*

Thawing fruit

➤ *see Fruit, Frozen, page 48*

Thawing meat

➤ *see Meat, page 71*

Thawing vegetables

➤ *see Cooking Frozen Vegetables, page 119*

Thyme

➤ *see Herbs, Drying, page 55*

Timing

The length of time foods take to cook depends on their size, shape, density, the amount of fat and sugar and even the shape and size of the dish.

➤ *see also Cooking Times, page 31, Dishes, page 37, and Quantities, page 91*

Toast

You can't make toast in the microwave but once cooked it can be topped with beans, cheese, etc., then heated in the oven.

To reheat cold toast, place on a sheet of kitchen paper (paper towel) and microwave on High for 10–20 seconds.

➤ *see also Baked Beans, page 11, Cheese, page 26, and Welsh Rarebit, page 121*

Tomatoes

Skinning tomatoes   Many recipes call for skinned tomatoes. This can be done very simply by microwaving each tomato on High for 10–15 seconds. Leave to stand for 30 seconds, then peel off the skin.

Stewed tomatoes   Make a small cross cut in the round end of the tomatoes with a sharp knife. Place in a circle in a dish. Cover and microwave on High for 1–2 minutes until just cooked but still holding their shape. After 1 minute, check every 15 seconds. Stand for 2 minutes before serving.

Tomato sauce   Peel and chop an onion. Put on a large bowl with a knob of butter or 15 ml/1 tbsp olive oil. Microwave on High for 2–3 minutes, stirring twice. Add a 400 g/14 oz/large can of chopped tomatoes, 15 ml/ 1 tsp tomato purée (paste), a pinch of caster (superfine) sugar and a pinch of dried basil or oregano. Microwave on High for 3–5 minutes until bubbling and slightly reduced. Season to taste and use as required.

Tortillas, flour

➢ *see Pancakes, page 82*

Turkey

➢ *see Poultry and Game, pages 86–8*

Turning

It is important to turn and stir food during cooking to achieve more even distribution of the microwaves, particularly if you don't have a turntable (➢ *see below*) or paddles (➢ *see page 82*) in your oven.

Turnips

➢ *see Vegetables, pages 115–19*

Turntable

Many microwave ovens have a turntable attached to the base of the oven that turns automatically while the microwave is in operation. It keeps food turning to help more even distribution of the microwaves. It is still important to stir and rearrange food during cooking.

➢ *see also Hot and Cold Spots, page 56, Stirring, page 106, and Turning, above*

U

Undercooking

It is always better to undercook food in the microwave, then check and cook for a little longer if necessary.

Many dishes, such as fish, eggs, cakes and some puddings, in particular, may seem undercooked when you take them out but will complete cooking during standing time (➤ *see page 104*).

➤ *see also Cooking Times, page 31.*

Upside-down pudding

➤ *see Sponge Puddings, page 103*

Utensils

You can use metal utensils to stir food but NEVER leave them in the microwave. A spoon rest at the side of the cooker is a good idea.

A wooden spoon, however, can be left in a bowl of food that needs repeated stirring during microwaving. But do not leave for a long period of time as it will become hot and may burn. Also, make sure the spoon does not touch the top or sides of the oven during microwaving.

➤ *see also Dishes, page 37*

Vacherin

> *see Meringues, page 74*

Variable power

> *see Power Output Settings, page 89*

Veal

> *see Meat, pages 71–4*

Vegetables

Vegetables cook extremely well in the microwave, saving all the nutrients and colour as very little liquid is needed. The chart overleaf gives you the preparation and cooking times for most kinds of fresh vegetable. Cooking times will vary according to the quantity of vegetables and the output of your microwave. Always cook for the shortest time given, check, then cook in 30-second bursts until cooked to your liking. Remember they will continue to cook slightly during their standing time when they should be left covered and undisturbed.

As an added convenience, you can cook your vegetables in advance in serving dishes, then quickly reheat in the microwave before serving without loss of nutrients, colour or flavour.

For best results, follow these general rules:

- Keep water to a minimum (> *see chart overleaf*). But if you like your vegetables soft, add a little extra water and cook for a few seconds longer.
- Vegetables with a high water content, such as spinach, mushrooms and courgettes (zucchini), don't need any extra water. The water clinging to them after washing is sufficient. At most, add 30 ml/2 tbsp.
- Always pierce the skin of whole vegetables, like jacket potatoes, to prevent bursting.
- Cut vegetables into even-sized pieces for even cooking.
- Arrange with the most delicate parts towards the centre of the dish, e.g. the heads of broccoli or asparagus.
- Always cover vegetables – a casserole (Dutch oven) is ideal. This does not apply to jacket potatoes which should be wrapped individually in kitchen paper (paper towels).
- Stir gently or rearrange once during cooking for more even results.
- If you wish to add salt, do so at the end of cooking before leaving the vegetables to stand. Salting before cooking will toughen them.

Vegetable cooking times

Fresh vegetable/ quantity	Preparation and method	Cooking time and power level	Standing time
Artichokes, globe 450 g/1 lb	Twist off stalks and trim points of leaves. Arrange in a circle in a casserole dish (Dutch oven). Add 60 ml/ 4 tbsp water. Cover.	10–15 minutes on Medium-High. Rearrange twice during cooking.	4 minutes
Artichokes, Jerusalem 450 g/1 lb	Scrub or peel. Cut into chunks. Place in a casserole dish (Dutch oven). Add 60 ml/4 tbsp water. Cover.	6–8 minutes on High	3 minutes
Asparagus 450 g/1 lb	Trim off any woody stalks. Arrange in an even layer in a shallow dish. Add 60 ml/ 4 tbsp water. Cover.	5–9 minutes on High	3 minutes
Aubergines (eggplants) 1 medium	Trim off stalks and slice. Arrange in a shallow dish. Add 90 ml/6 tbsp water. Cover.	6–9 minutes on High	2 minutes
Beans, French (green) and runner 225 g/8 oz	Top and tail and leave whole, cut into short lengths or slice for runner beans. Place in a casserole. Add 90 ml/ 6 tbsp water. Cover.	6–10 minutes on High	4 minutes
Beans, broad (fava) 225 g/8 oz (shelled weight)	Shell and place in a casserole dish (Dutch oven). Add 60 ml/4 tbsp water. Cover.	4–6 minutes on High	4 minutes
Beetroot (red beets) 4 medium	Wash but do not peel. Place whole in a dish. Cover with boiling water, then a lid.	16–24 minutes on Medium-High, turning once or twice.	8 minutes
Broccoli 225 g/8 oz	Separate into florets. Trim tough stalks. Arrange in a circle in a dish, heads to the centre. Add 45 ml/3 tbsp water. Cover.	6–9 minutes on High	3 minutes
Brussels sprouts 225 g/8 oz	Trim. Place in a casserole dish (Dutch oven). Add 45 ml/3 tbsp water.	6–9 minutes on High	3 minutes
Cabbage 1 medium	Remove outer leaves and any thick stalks. Shred. Place in a casserole dish (Dutch oven). Add 45 ml/3 tbsp water. Cover.	6–9 minutes on High, stirring twice.	3 minutes
Carrots 450 g/1 lb	Peel or scrape and slice or cut into matchsticks. Add 45 ml/3 tbsp water. Cover.	8–12 minutes on High	3 minutes

Fresh vegetable/ quantity	Preparation and method	Cooking time and power level	Standing time
Cauliflower 1 medium	Separate into florets, discarding any thick stalk. Arrange in a round dish, heads to the centre. Add 90 ml/6 tbsp water. Cover.	8–12 minutes on High	4 minutes
Celeriac (celery root) 1 medium	Peel and cut into matchsticks. Place in a casserole dish (Dutch oven) and add 60 ml/4 tbsp water and 5 ml/1 tsp lemon juice.	6–9 minutes on High, stirring twice.	3 minutes
Celery 1 head	Scrub, then slice. Place in a casserole dish (Dutch oven) with 45 ml/3 tbsp water. Cover.	7–10 minutes on High, stirring twice.	2 minutes
Corn on the cob 2 cobs	Remove husks and silks. Trim stalks. Place in a dish and add 45 ml/3 tbsp water. Cover. Cook 2 cobs at a time, or wrap individually in lightly buttered greaseproof (waxed) paper and place on the turntable.	5–9 minutes on High, turning once.	2 minutes
Courgettes (zucchini) 2 medium	Trim ends, then slice. Arrange in a dish. Add 30 ml/2 tbsp water. Cover.	4–6 minutes on High, stirring twice.	3 minutes
Fennel 1 head	Trim the feathery fronds and reserve for garnish. Cut into slices or small wedges. Place in a dish and add 60 ml/ 4 tbsp water. Cover.	4–6 minutes on High, stirring twice.	2 minutes
Leeks 2 medium	Trim, slice and wash very thoroughly. Place in a casserole dish (Dutch oven) and add 45 ml/3 tbsp water. Cover.	4–7 minutes on High	2 minutes
Mangetout (snow peas) 225 g/8 oz	Top and tail but leave whole. Place in a casserole dish (Dutch oven). Add 60 ml/ 4 tbsp water. Cover.	4–6 minutes on High, stirring once.	2 minutes
Marrow (squash) 1 small	Peel and slice or dice, discarding seeds (pits). Place in a casserole dish (Dutch oven). Add 30 ml/2 tbsp water. Cover.	5–8 minutes on High, stirring twice.	3 minutes
Onions 225 g/8 oz	Peel and leave whole, if small, or chop and slice. Place in a casserole dish (Dutch oven) and add 45 ml/3 tbsp water. Cover.	3–7 minutes on High, stirring once or twice.	2 minutes

Stuffed marrow 10 min. on High. (handwritten annotation)

Fresh vegetable/ quantity	Preparation and method	Cooking time and power level	Standing time
Parsnips 2 medium	Peel and slice. Place in a casserole dish (Dutch oven). Add 60 ml/4 tbsp water. Cover.	5–8 minutes on High	3 minutes
Peas 225 g/8 oz shelled weight	Shell and place in a casserole dish (Dutch oven). Add 45 ml/3 tbsp water and a sprig of mint.	4–6 minutes on High, stirring twice.	2 minutes
Potatoes, baked 2 large	Scrub and prick with a fork. Wrap in kitchen paper (paper towels). Arrange in a circle on the turntable.	8–10 minutes on High, turning once.	4 minutes, wrapped in a cloth or foil.
Potatoes, boiled 450 g/1 lb	Scrub or peel, leave new ones whole or cut into even-sizd pieces. Place in a casserole dish (Dutch oven), add a sprig of mint, if new. Add 45 ml/3 tbsp water. Cover.	8–12 minutes on High, stirring once or twice.	3 minutes
Spinach 225 g/8 oz	Wash well, discarding any thick stalks. Place in a dish with no extra water. Cover.	5–8 minutes on High, stirring once.	2 minutes
Spring (collard) greens 450 g/1 lb	Wash well, discard any thick stalks and shred. Place in a casserole dish (Dutch oven) and add 45 ml/3 tbsp water. Cover.	6–10 minutes on High, stirring twice.	3 minutes
Sweet potatoes 450 g/1 lb	Peel and cut into chunks. Place in a casserole dish (Dutch oven). Add 60 ml/ 4 tbsp water. Cover.	8–12 minutes on High, stirring once or twice.	3 minutes
Swede (rutabaga) 1 medium	Peel and dice. Place in a casserole dish (Dutch oven). Add 60 ml/4 tbsp water.	5–8 minutes on High, stirring once or twice.	3 minutes
Turnips 450 g/1 lb	Peel and leave whole if small or dice. Place in a casserole dish (Dutch oven) and add 60 ml/4 tbsp water.	5–8 minutes on High, stirring once or twice.	3 minutes
Yams 450 g/1 lb	Prepare as for sweet potatoes.	5–8 minutes on High, stirring once or twice.	3 minutes

Peppers - stuffed with cooked filling
8 min at High (up to 4 veg.)

Blanching vegetables Vegetables can be blanched in the microwave before freezing. Put up to 450 g/1 lb of the prepared vegetable in a large bowl with 60 ml/4 tbsp water. Cook on High for 2 minutes. Stir and cook for a further 1–2 minutes, depending on the quantity of vegetables and the output of your oven, until the vegetables are hot. Drain immediately and plunge into ice-cold water. Drain again, pack, label and freeze in your usual way.

Cooking frozen vegetables It is not generally necessary to thaw vegetables before cooking. For best results when cooking frozen vegetables, follow these general rules:

- Cook on High instead of Medium-Low.
- Allow an extra 1–2 minutes' cooking time compared with fresh (➤ *see Vegetable Cooking Times, pages 116–18*).
- Home-frozen vegetables will take a little longer to cook than commercially prepared ones.
- No added water is necessary.
- Always use a covered dish.
- To cook more than 225 g/8 oz frozen vegetables, do it in two batches.
- If the vegetables are in a block, break up gently as soon as possible, and stir once or twice to distribute the heat more evenly.
- If cooking whole bags of commercially frozen vegetables, there is no need to empty them into a container. Snip the corner off the bag and place in the oven. Gently flex or shake the bag once or twice during cooking to loosen the contents and distribute the heat more evenly. Remove with oven gloves as the bag will soften and get very hot. Pour off any liquid before serving.

Cooking several vegetables at once You usually want more than one vegetable with a meal. If you have a divided microwave dish, this is ideal. But you can arrange up to three small dishes in the cooker at one time. Start with the vegetable that takes the longest, then add the others a little later. For instance, if you are cooking new potatoes, carrots and courgettes (zucchini), put the potatoes in first and start to cook them, add the carrots after a minute or two, then the courgettes. To compensate for the extra quantity of food in the microwave (which will affect the cooking time), add on 1–2 minutes at the end.

Venison

Venison needs careful cooking and is best marinated and cooked conventionally. However, it can be cooked like hare.

➤ *see also Poultry and Game, pages 86–8*

Victoria sandwich

➤ *see Cakes, Sponge, page 23*

Vinegar

Flavoured vinegar   Use red wine, white wine, distilled white or cider vinegar. Pour into a bowl and add a large sprig of herbs of your choice or a few fresh chillis and peppercorns. Cover and microwave on High for 1–2 minutes until the vinegar is warm but not hot. Leave until completely cold. Pour into an airtight container (or the original vinegar bottle), including the herbs or chillis. Seal tightly and store in a cool, dark place for at least 2 weeks before using.

Spiced vinegar   Add 5 ml/1 tsp pickling spice to 300 ml/½ pt/1¼ cups malt vinegar in a bowl or glass bottle (with no metal tops). Microwave on High until bubbles appear, but do not boil. Leave to stand for 10 minutes to infuse. Either use straight away for picking onions etc., or leave until completely cold, then store in a dark place until ready for use.

Vol-au-vents

You cannot cook vol-au-vents in the microwave but they reheat well when cooked and filled. Arrange on kitchen paper (paper towels) on a plate in a circle. Microwave on High, checking every 10–15 seconds until hot through, no longer. If overcooked they will be very soggy.

Water

It is not practical to use a microwave for boiling more than 300 ml/½ pt/ 1¼ cups water (an individual mugful to make a drink, for instance). Larger quantities boil more quickly in a kettle or saucepan with a lid on the conventional cooker.

When using a microwave you need less water or other cooking liquid than when cooking conventionally.

➤ *see also Recipe Conversion, page 92*

Wattage

This is the measure of the power output of your oven.

➤ *see also Power Output Settings, page 89*

Waxed paper

➤ *see Greaseproof Paper, page 53*

Welsh rarebit

Mash a knob of butter or margarine with 45 ml/3 tbsp grated Cheddar cheese, 10 ml/2 tsp beer, cider or apple juice, a good pinch each of mustard powder, salt and freshly ground black pepper. Make a piece of toast. Spread the cheese mixture on top. Place on a plate. Microwave on High for 20–30 seconds until melted. Serve straight away.

Whiting

➤ *see Fish, page 43*

Wine

To bring cold red wine to room temperature, pour into a large jug or glass carafe. Microwave on High for 10–15 seconds. Stir and leave to stand for 5 minutes. Either pour back into the bottle or serve from the carafe.

➤ *see also Mulled Wine, page 77*

Xmas cake

➤ *see Christmas Cake, page 23*

Xmas pudding

➤ *see Christmas Pudding, page 28*

Yams

> *see Vegetables, pages 115–19*

Yoghurt

You can make delicious, smooth yoghurt with the help of the microwave. Pour 500 ml/17 fl oz/2¼ cups UHT milk in a clean bowl, previously rinsed in boiling water. Microwave on Medium for 1 minute or until blood heat (neither hot or cold to the touch). Whisk in 150 ml/¼ pt/⅔ cup plain yoghurt. Pour into a clean vacuum flask and seal. Leave to stand, undisturbed, for several hours or overnight until set. Turn into a clean container, cover and store in the fridge.

Yorkshire puddings

You cannot make Yorkshire puddings successfully in the microwave but you can reheat them. Put 4–6 puddings in a circle on a sheet of kitchen paper (paper towel) on a plate. Microwave on High for 20–40 seconds.

Z

Zabaglione

Whisk together 1 egg, 15 ml/1 tbsp caster (superfine) sugar and 25 ml/
1½ tbsp dry or medium sherry. Cook for 20 seconds on Medium. Whisk
again. Cook for about 1 minute, in 10-second blasts, whisking well after
each blast until thick and foamy. Pour into wine goblets and serve
straight away with sponge (lady) fingers. Serves 2.

Zest

If you have oranges, lemons or limes that need using up, finely grate the
rind and spread evenly on a plate. Put a small cup of water beside them to
absorb some of the energy. Microwave on High, stirring and testing every
minute, until the zest has completely dried out. Leave to stand for several
hours or overnight, then store in an airtight container. Use to flavour
breads, biscuits (cookies), cakes, puddings and sauces. (The juice may be
squeezed and frozen in ice cube trays.)

Zucchini

> see Courgettes, page 33, and Vegetables, pages 115–19